Third Edition

The Business of Ecotourism

The Complete Guide for Nature and Culture-Based Tourism Operators

Carol Patterson

Foreword by
Delia & Mark Owens
Owens Foundation for Wildlife Conservation

Order this book online at www.trafford.com
or email orders@trafford.com

Most Trafford titles are also available at major online book retailers.

Print information available on the last page.

ISBN: 978-1-4251-1724-5 (sc)
ISBN: 978-1-4251-2707-7 (e)

Trafford rev. 01/16/2019

 www.trafford.com

North America & international
toll-free: 1 888 232 4444 (USA & Canada)
fax: 812 355 4082

This book is dedicated to my parents,
who taught me that anything is possible.

TABLE OF CONTENTS

FOREWORD

by Delia and Mark Owens

In 1974, outfitted with only two sleeping bags, a few supplies, and a third-hand Land Rover, we ventured into the vast Kalahari Desert of Botswana as two wide-eyed, inexperienced wildlife biologists to study desert lions and hyenas. The only two people, except for a few Bushmen, in an area the size of Ireland, we developed unique relationships with these large and secretive carnivores. After several years we could sit with wild lions under scrawny Acacia trees, or among the romping cubs at the hyena den. We were fortunate to make fascinating discoveries about the natural history of these magnificent species.

We stayed in the Kalahari seven years, living in tents, rationing water, surviving the heat. It was the most wondrous of study areas for any scientist - free, wild, remote, and full of undiscovered treasures. But in one season all of that changed. A prolonged and scorching drought gripped the desert in the late 1970s, and stimulated the wildebeest to migrate north toward natural watering points they had used for thousands of years in such severe conditions. The wildebeest could deal with drought and dust, but in their path lay a five hundred mile fence erected to control a cattle disease that had never been recorded in the Kalahari. A quarter of a million wildebeest died only a few miles from the lake, and the population, formerly the second largest in Africa, has never recovered.

This was a clear case of the economic value of cattle being placed above that a wild species. But cattle ranches in these dry dunes only survived for a few years. Once the wells ran dry and the grasses were overgrazed, the ranchers moved on to other areas. The wildebeest would have survived indefinitely if they had been allowed to migrate to water. But the wildebeest were gone; a few years later so were the cattle.

The message was as clear and bright as the stars of the desert sky. In some natural environments, wild animals can have more economic value in the long term through tourism, or other wildlife related industries, than can domestic stock not adapted to the habitat. We wrote a proposal, recommending that the Kalahari Game Reserve be developed for tourism that would benefit local people. But this was in the early 1980s, and the concept of ecotourism was as exotic as cattle in the desert.

We traveled overland to Zambia to search for a new study area. Bashing through the outback of the southern Kafue National Park we saw only five wild animals in five days. At night around our campfire we heard the poachers' guns, and every dawn we found meat racks used to dry illegal game meat. After days of grueling cross-country adventure, we reach northern Kafue, which had several tourism safari camps nestled in deep bush along the rivers. Here the impala and puku continued to graze as we drove past, hippos winked at us, and Vervet monkeys hopped on our truck. The only difference between northern and southern Kafue was one thing - tourism. The presence of the safari camps, their guides, operators, and clients was a deterrent to poachers. In addition the camps provided jobs for many rural Africans in an area where no other industries existed. This experience convinced us more than ever that ecotourism, developed properly, can benefit wildlife and people in many regions of the earth.

We set out to demonstrate that involving local people in conservation can improve the living standards of villagers and the survival rate of wildlife. In 1986 poachers were shooting one thousand elephants a year in North Luangwa National Park in Zambia; poaching was the number one industry in the province. We set up a program to train and finance rural villagers to be carpenters, fish farmers, millers, bee keepers, and shop keepers, as alternatives to poaching. We encouraged a few tour operators to develop low-impact walking safaris in the park. We worked with the government of Zambia to design a management plan for the park that required tourism to benefit local people. In 1996 no elephants were shot in North Luangwa. It took ten years, but it worked.

We have lived in Africa for more than two decades now, and have witnessed the needless elimination of wildlife in many wilderness areas in favor of exotic development schemes. We have also seen some remarkable victories evolve from the African dust. This book discusses one of those success stories.

One of the most successful strategies for saving wildlife populations is to give them economic value and therefore, a voice with decision makers. This economic value can be provided, under proper circumstances, through ecotourism, where small groups of tourists visit sensitive environments and provide long-term benefits to local people from increased revenue, jobs, and small industries. These opportunities are not only necessary for the livelihood of rural people, but this renewed relationship between man and wildlife is nourishing a long lasting respect by man for his wild neighbors. Tourists also benefit by learning about wildlife management issues.

"Ecotourism" has become a buzz word, and it must not be thought of as the solution to all the problems of the wild. But it can, and is, contributing to the conservation of natural resources in numerous regions of our planet. *The Business of Ecotourism* is a tool that you can use to establish a viable and sustainable tourism enterprise. It focuses on the planning, marketing, and operational requirements unique to ecotourism, and provides practical advice so the new or experienced can succeed in this often challenging field.

Most importantly, *The Business of Ecotourism* encourages people entering the field of ecotourism to consider their personal values with respect to wildlife. This is essential, because we have witnessed cases in which ecotourism, through its success, has compromised conservation for the sake of increased economic returns. Balancing financial gain and sound conservation practices, so that both the business and the environment flourishes, is not only the ultimate reward, it should be considered a pledge to the earth before the first tent is ever erected on virgin soil. Reports on the adverse effects of "ecotourism" on wildlife populations are already being filed against this relatively new industry. But whether it is too many safari trucks surrounding a hunting cheetah or too many hands touching a porpoise, this is not bad ecotourism - this is not ecotourism at all. If you follow this trail, never take the "eco" out of the tourism.

True naturalists are as excited about the smallest spores on the ferns of the rain forest as they are about the grueling fight of two bull elephants. We wish for success with your ecotourism endeavor, but ask that you place your book carefully with every step on earth's paths that are yet wild.

Delia and Mark Owens
June 1997
Luangwa Valley, Zambia

INTRODUCTION

Since the dawn of mankind, people have traveled seasonally in search of food and better living conditions. The Twentieth Century brought an era where people were able to travel for pleasure. While initially travel was limited to the wealthy, since World War II, working class people can travel as never before. This change in our society has led to the birth of a major industry - tourism, and promises to be the fastest growing industry on the planet. Tourism is now undergoing another revolution.

While taking more trips than ever in history, people are also seeking enriching adventures in their leisure and travel. They are looking for experiences in nature, opportunities to discover foreign cultures, and personal challenges and discoveries. One of the off-shoots of this quest has been the emergence of new travel markets focused on nature, culture, and adventure. Called by many names - ecotourism, adventure travel, nature tourism, or sustainable tourism - these new areas are the fastest-growing segments of the tourism industry. For the entrepreneur, resource manager, or community group, there are exciting opportunities, and potential pitfalls, ahead.

Being prepared for these opportunities means knowing how to design an ecotourism product. It requires skill in marketing because these new tourists are more demanding. "Walking the green walk" means you need to plan your operations so Mother Earth is no worse off because of your ecotourism business. Recruiting and retaining the right guides and support staff will be critical in meeting visitor expectations. Implementing sound financial management strategies is also important, as sustainability on a business level means making enough profit seasonally to pay the bills.

You may think with so many opportunities you can start an ecotourism or nature tourism business without assistance and succeed. While there is such a thing as beginner's luck, there are many more cases of lost savings, wasted business opportunities, and broken dreams. Even people who have a proven track record in the tourism industry will find *The Business of Ecotourism* a shortcut to learning what the ecotourist or nature traveler is looking for. Instructors will find the book a valuable teaching tool for classes interested in sustainable tourism.

This book was written as a step-by-step manual to guide people through the process of creating and building a successful ecotourism operation. It provides sound business advice while focusing on the unique features of operating an ecotourism business.

Examples show how others have made it in this exciting field. Checklists, planning schedules, and a workbook are also included to help you plan and build your ecotourism venture. *The Business of Ecotourism* uses examples from actual people and ecotourism businesses to illustrate key points. Sample forms help you work along with the book and a workbook is provided in Appendix A so you can start working without delay.

This book is divided into several sections, each corresponding to a major functional area in an ecotourism venture. Chapters 1 through 3 provide an industry overview and its most unique features. These chapters will help you decide if ecotourism is the right business for you.

Marketing and product development are the focus of chapters 4 through 6. Learning to position your ecotourism product in the eyes of potential customers is critical if your business is to survive. There is fierce competition locally and globally for travel dollars. You will need to build a marketing plan with the diligence of a military leader planning a battle. *The Business of Ecotourism* will walk you through this important phase in detail.

Business operations are covered in Chapters 7 through 10. Because so many ecotourism activities occur in the wild and depend upon person-to-person interaction, you need to develop environmentally-sound business policies and procedures. Training staff and orienting customers will become important parts of your business focus. Taking care of customers and the environment will force you to consider safety and property loss issues.

The need to turn your ideas into action, and to do so consistently well into the future, is the focus of Chapters 11 and 12. A business plan will take your ideas and help you articulate your plans in a way that will increase staff or investor support. It will also keep your goals clear in your mind once you have begun everyday operations.

Industry standards and the need to set benchmarks for environmentally-responsible tourism set the tone for the closing of the book. Delivering your first ecotourism trip may be relatively easy. Making sure the one-thousandth trip is delivered to the same standard is the tricky part. The need for industry standards or certification and its current status is discussed as we look to the future.

Ecotourism can be a viable and satisfying way of balancing environmental preservation with cultural and economic well-being. Taking advantage of its promise means careful planning, good business skills, and a love of nature. Working as an ecotourism operator and as a part of the larger industry will mean adherence to higher principles and standards than the minimums required by government regulations. While the challenges are many, the rewards are even greater.

May all your trips be successful ones and may this book help you in your quest for the ultimate travel experience.

1 UNDERSTANDING THE ECOTOURISM INDUSTRY

ECOTOURISM DEFINITIONS

While no accepted definition of ecotourism exists, a commonly-used definition is one developed by The International Ecotourism Society (formerly known as The Ecotourism Society.) It states, "Ecotourism is responsible travel to natural areas which conserves the environment and improves the welfare of local people"[1].

This definition suggests several criteria for evaluating whether your venture is part of the ecotourism industry. The travel experience would be one, based upon nature, two, contribute to the conservation of the environment, three, contribute culturally and economically to the local economy. Some would also suggest another criterion - that your clients have a learning experience.

What business would be classified as ecotourism? Does a tour operator who uses a helicopter to reach wilderness areas provide an ecotourism experience? Some environmental groups object strongly to the use of helicopters, while supporters claim they reduce impacts on the environment. Is a bus tour company that offers nature-based tours, makes a donation to environmental projects, and hires local people, an ecotourism operator?

It is not the size of the operation nor the type of activity that defines ecotourism but the principles behind the business.

Clearly, if you evaluate any tourism, you find there are environmental impacts. The best we can do is to minimize the impact of our visitation. Perhaps it is not the size of the operation nor the type of activity that defines ecotourism but the principles behind the business. Some people have turned to other definitions to develop a more workable term. "Nature-based tourism" is a phrase that is becoming more common and refers to all tourism that relies on the natural environment [2].

"Adventure tourism" is "an outdoor leisure activity that takes place in unusual, exotic, remote or wilderness destinations, involves some form of unconventional means of transportation, and tends to be associated with low or high levels of activity"[3].

The main difference between nature-based, adventure, and ecotourism is the motivation or ethic behind the tourism product. All of these experiences require nature; the difference is in the care taken with the environment and the effort to help the local economy.

1

The terms "responsible" or "sustainable" tourism express the intent behind the tourism experience.

An adventure traveler who climbs Mt. Everest and leaves garbage behind or uses scarce firewood is not an ecotourist. An adventure traveler who climbs Mt. Everest and practices low impact camping most likely *would* be an ecotourist. Some nature-based tourism products in developing countries are not considered ecotourism because they do not improve the welfare of local people. As an example, much of the money generated from wildlife safaris in east Africa does not directly benefit the tribal people who were displaced when the parks were created.

Other terminology includes "responsible" or "sustainable tourism". This expresses the *intent* under which the tourism was undertaken. One of the most comprehensive studies grappled with the definition of ecotourism and elected to survey people on a description of the travel experience as opposed to using the term "ecotourism". The definition used for the study was "vacations where the traveler would experience nature, adventure, or cultural experiences in the countryside" [4].

If all this leaves you wondering if your business is part of ecotourism, perhaps the simplest test is to evaluate your business against the characteristics in figure 1-1. If your business has many of these characteristics, it is probably an ecotourism business.

Evaluate your business against these characteristics to see if it can be considered an ecotourism business.

FIGURE 1-1   **CHARACTERISTICS OF AN ECOTOURISM BUSINESS**
· Uses low impact camping and recreation techniques · Limits visitation to areas, either by limiting group size and/or by the number of groups taken to an area in a season · Supports the work of conservation groups preserving the natural area on which the experience is based · Orients customers on the region to be visited · Hires local people and buys supplies locally, where possible · Recognises that nature is a central element to the tourist experience · Uses guides trained in interpretation of scientific or natural history · Ensures that wildlife is not harassed · Respects the privacy and culture of local people

INDUSTRY GROWTH

The lack of definition for ecotourism has led to difficulty in collecting statistical information on this industry segment and in forming associations to promote destinations and activities. However, the World Tourism Organization (WTO) in 1989 found that nature travel represented seven percent of all travel [5]. This is a large number, given that tourism world-wide in 1995 was $3.4 trillion in gross output [6]. A Canadian study found a potential ecotourism market of 13.2 million travelers in only seven major metropolitan areas in Canada and the United States [7].

Wildlife recreationists have been identified as a large, growing, and important market segment. A 2001 study by the U.S. Fish and Wildlife Service and the U.S. Census Bureau showed that non-consumptive wildlife recreationists represented $38.4 billion annually in economic activity [8].

Tourism as a whole is forecast to grow by an average 4.1 percent annually through 1990 to 2020 [9]. Nature tourism is projected to grow much faster. Many nature tourism operators have experienced double-digit growth in recent years. The increase in tourism in countries such as Costa Rica and Nepal, where the tourism product is based upon an exotic nature experience, has been dramatic.

ECOTOURISM PRODUCTS

The growth of the nature-based tourism market, combined with significant trip expenditures, has stimulated the development of nature-tourism operators. Some operators have existing businesses and are looking to diversify into ecotourism. For example, commercial outfitters may add wildlife photography trips to increase business during "shoulder" seasons. Other businesses may be started in response to the demand for a certain product, for example, tours of bird staging areas or lodges that provide contact with indigenous cultures. North American trip wholesalers search for operators who offer a nature experience for high-yield tourists from Europe and Japan.

Your choice of nature, cultural, or soft adventure tourism venture is limited only by your imagination.

Ecotourism and nature-based tourism products can be found in every state and province in North America. Guide books provide ecotourists with suggestions on destinations and tour operators. Good examples of these guides are *Earth Trips: A Guide To Nature Travel On A Fragile Planet* by Dwight Holing or *Ecotours And Nature Getaways: A Guide To Environmental Vacations Around The World* by Carole Berglie and Alice M. Geffen.

Numerous web sites have been developed to help people plan their next trip. Some of these are geared towards specialty markets such as ecotourism or adventure travel.

When developing your ecotourism product, you will only be limited by your imagination. Business owners have shown considerable creativity in developing experiences that appeal to the tourist. In addition to canoeing, walking, hiking, kayaking, camping, and rafting, you will find businesses offering a chance to see wildlife in natural settings. There is polar bear watching in Churchill, Manitoba, gorilla treks in east Africa, wolf tracking in the Rockies, and turtle observation in Florida, to name a few. Others may include nature hikes offered to resort guests and raptor flying demonstrations at ski hills in the summer months.

Culture and history may be the main attraction of a product. Museums or displays of aboriginal culture are very popular with North American and European travelers as are tours of historical sites. Paleontology and archaeology have formed the basis for tours as people help excavate sites looking for dinosaur remains, and prehistoric or historic settlements. Zoological parks and aquariums provide an orientation to wild environments and offer natural history trips that increase people's understanding of ecosystems. Hotel owners are producing wildlife-viewing guides and providing staff training in wildlife viewing. For people who want to be immersed in nature, there are back-country cabins, rain forest lodges, and tented camps.

Ideas for ecotourism products can stem from every component of the tourism industry.

Table 1-1 illustrates the range of products and services where ecotourism can be found and provides specific examples for each category. Every component of the tourism industry from accommodations to touring to food services can spawn a product idea that will allow a business or individual to enter the ecotourism industry.

Many people will think of tours when contemplating ecotourism opportunities and this has been the most visible aspect of ecotourism to date. Tour operators have provided hiking, biking, canoeing, climbing, photography, and wildlife-viewing tours, among others. Tour operators have led people from other parts of the world on tours in their host communities (in-bound tours) and taken people from local communities on tours of distant lands (out-bound tours).

Becoming a tour operator or tour packager (someone who combines tour products and sells them as a package) has the advantage of being relatively easy to start. Financing requirements are considerably less than for building an attraction or back-country lodge. Someone with a good knowledge of local resources and the ability to market aggressively can find this an excellent way to enter the ecotourism industry.

Other options you may consider are the provision of services, from guiding and interpretation to equipment rental. Although competition for interpretation business can be fierce, it is an area where relatively little capital is required and the often seasonal nature of the business can leave time to pursue other opportunities.

Establishing a lodge or other accommodation may be very attractive. The market for these facilities is quite strong, but there is considerable effort required to obtain regulatory approvals and financing. With proper planning and sufficient perseverance, this can be a very rewarding entry into ecotourism.

Entering the retail industry may not occur to you, but ecotourists spend money just like other travelers. If you can provide high-quality clothing or equipment, or

TABLE 1-1 **TYPES OF ECOTOURISM VENTURES**		
Category of Ecotourism Product	**Sub-Categories**	**Examples**
Tour Packages	In-bound Out-bound Culture-based Nature-based Adventure-based Historical Educational	Europeans biking through the Napa Valley New Yorkers taking a wildlife safari in South Africa Tour of several native communities Birdwatching walk Trekking in Nepal Tour of historic fort Tour of reclaimed logging sites
Festivals	Wildlife	Festival celebrating migration of sandhill cranes
Accommodations	Lodges Bed and Breakfasts Tented camp	Backcountry lodge offering hiking/cross country skiing Bed and Breakfast with birdwatching opportunities Tented river camp offering canoe trips
Guiding Services	Interpretative talks Step on services Safety orientation Interpretative activities Dramatic presentations	Evening horticultural talk Cultural interpretation for tour bus Bear safety courses Guided day hike of geological formations Recreation of historical event at national monument
Attractions	Zoos, Aquariums Museums Historic sites and parks	Internationally accredited zoo Eco-museum 19th century town
Non-Profit Associations	Environmental Conservation Historical Cultural	Natural history hike Wildlife rescue center Recreation of special celebration or day
Food Services	Restaurants Catering Banquets	Feature organic meals for visiting birdwatchers Picnic lunches for day hikes Aboriginal dinner theater
Retail	Equipment rental/sales Books Arts and crafts	Optical sales e.g. binoculars, scopes Wildlife viewing guides Indigenous craft co-op for authentic trip mementos
Transportation	Automotive rentals Aircraft charters/rentals Animal Boat	Van rentals for tour operators Helicopter transport of ecotourists to remote camps Llama transport of camping equipment Pangas for whalewatching

authentic mementos representing your region, you should be able to generate considerable revenue from ecotourism.

There are more unconventional ways to enter ecotourism. If you have an interest in rescuing wildlife, ecotourism may provide a way of subsidizing your conservation activities. Some wildlife rescue centers have been approached for private tours before they have opened their doors to the public. Non-profit organizations such as zoos and conservation groups are looking at ecotourism activities to fulfill their mission to educate people on nature, and to supplement government grants. If you can find a way to link non-profit organizations with nature or cultural travel, there may be an opportunity to create an ecotourism product.

WHO ARE THE ECOTOURISTS?

Much of the success of an ecotourism business will revolve around your ability to understand market segments and structure your product offering to meet their needs. Few studies have been done on ecotourism per se; however, market studies on related areas may be helpful. As a guide, some of the terms found in literature that are relevant to ecotourism are shown in figure 1-2.

If we look at the demographic information and travel motivators from a variety of sources, we notice some commonalties. This information will help you understand your clients, and develop and market your product accordingly.

FIGURE 1-2 **TERMS THAT MAY BE ASSOCIATED WITH ECOTOURISM**	
Nature tourism	Soft adventure tourism
Nature-based tourism	Responsible tourism
Avitourism (bird watching)	Environmentally sensitive tourism
Green tourism	Low impact tourism
Cultural tourism	Sustainable tourism
Historical tourism	Ethical tourism
Special interest travel	Environmental tourism
Wildlife recreation	Educational tourism
Safari travel	Rural tourism
Adventure tourism	Wilderness tourism

Age is not a significant factor among ecotourism participants.

AGE - Ecotourists span a wide range of ages. This is to be expected, given the range of activities in ecotourism experiences. Activities that are demanding physically tend to attract younger travelers. A study done by Tourism Canada found the typical adventure traveler was a male and between 20 and 44 years of age [10].

Where activities are less strenuous, ages are higher. The Ecotourism Society Fact Sheet Collection suggests a general ecotourist profile is 35 to 54 years of age, with college education or above, and traveling as a couple [11]. This was supported by the ecotourism market assessment done for British Columbia and Alberta, which found the 25 to 54 age group predominated this type of travel [12]. A specialty tourist study done by Sorenson and Cresson found special interest tourists were in their 40s or 50s [13]. Bird watchers tend to be older than other tourists. A survey of the American Birding Association found the average age was 50.6 years, the majority in the 40 to 49 age bracket [14].

Recent surveys done with visitors to Florida and Texas show that while users of the Great Texas Coastal Birding Trail average 60 years of age[15], those people undertaking nature tourism activities in Florida are younger with 24.9 to 26 % coming from the 25-34 age group, and 30.5 to 36.5 % coming from the 35 to 49 age groups[16]. This may be due to the difference in trip focus; birders as a group tend to be more heavily represented by people from older age groups. When a variety of activities is introduced, the ages of trip participants tend to be younger. This was found in a recent study by the Travel Industry of America, which showed that 20% of bird and wildlife watchers, were over 55, a greater proportion than one would find in the overall population. The remaining bird and animal viewers were Boomers (35-54 years of age) 43%, and suprisingly, 37% were Generation Xers (age 18-34). If a more active sport such as hiking was examined, the Travel Industry of America found that most participants were Boomers (47%) followed closely by Generation Xers (41%) [17].

Ecotourists are generally well-educated and possess a higher level of income.

EDUCATION AND INCOME - Ecotourists are generally well educated. The Ecotourism Society Fact Sheet Collection shows that most ecotourists have a college education or above. The study of special interest tourists by Sorenson & Cresson found that survey respondents had a college degree or post graduate degree. The American Birding Association Survey found that 84 percent of respondents had a college degree. A survey done of users of the Great Texas Coastal Birding Trail show that users have an average of 17 years of education [18]. The Travel Industry of America found in their 1997 survey of adventure travelers that seven in ten soft adventure travelers have attended some college[19] .

This high level of education has several implications for developing your business. A higher level of education often generates a high level of income. This means you are dealing with a more sophisticated and informed audience. Clients place a value on learning in their lives that can carry through to their travel experiences. Providing knowledgeable guides and opportunity for discovery become very important in meeting the needs of these tourists.

Not all market surveys have gathered information on income, but it is generally believed that ecotourists possess a high level of income. This has been borne out by a number of studies. The American Birding Association 1991 survey found an average annual income of $50,520 [20]. A study done on Canadian ecotourists to Costa Rica in 1992 found an annual household income of $CDN 70,000 [21]. A Point Pelee Birding survey of avitourists found an annual household income of $57,175 [22]. Visit Florida's survey of nature tourists found slightly less correlation between household income and interest in nature travel than they expected, a possible explanation for this would be the low cost of entry for the variety of nature tourism activities covered in the survey[23].

Consistent with the higher income is high expenditures on nature-related travel. The ecotourism market demand assessment done for Alberta and British Columbia found that better than one-third of ecotourists spent over $CDN 1,500 per ecotourism trip [24]. The American Birding Association found that its members spend on average $4,623 on trips and equipment each year[25]. A 1999 survey of birdwatchers using the Great Texas Coastal Birding Trail found travelers spent $684 when visiting the trail[26]. For more details on their purchasing behavior see Figure 1-3. A Canadian study of ecotourists to Costa Rica found that $CDN 5,526 average was spent each year on travel [27]. If we look at adventure travelers, the Travel Industry of America found that hard adventure travelers spent $465 per trip, soft adventure travelers, $325 per trip[28].

There is an almost even split among male and female ecotourists.

GENDER - As with other demographic factors, gender varies among the surveys consulted and the trip activities. Many surveys show almost an even split among men and women. A 1988 World Wildlife Fund airport survey of nature tourists found that 51% were men and 49% were women [29]. The 2001 National Survey of Fishing, Hunting, and Wildlife-Associated Recreation found 46 percent of participants in wildlife viewing were men and 54% were women [30]. The Tourism Canada survey of adventure tourists found 54.4% were men and 45.6% were women [31]. Some birding surveys show a higher percentage of men participants. The Point Pelee Birding Survey found 59% men participants [32].

These surveys do not show the gender differences that occur by activity or trip duration. In informal discussions with ecotourism operators, many nature-viewing trips and hiking trips of several days duration appear to have a high percentage of women. It is important to keep the preferences of both genders in mind when developing your ecotourism product.

GROUP COMPOSITION - The Ecotourism Society Fact Sheet lists travel as a couple as a general characteristic [33]. The World Wildlife Fund airport survey found that approximately one-third of respondents traveled with family, the remainder of the respondents were split almost evenly among solo travel, travel with friends or a colleague, and travel with a tour [34].

FIGURE 1- 3 **THEY BUILT IT - WHO CAME?**
A Survey of Visitors to the Great Coastal Texas Birding Trail

---

Texas broke new ground several years back with its plans for a community-based tourism attraction ¾ the Great Texas Coastal Birding Trail (GTCBT.) The trail linked more than 300 sites with birdwatching opportunities along the central Texas coast. Maps and signage were drawn up and the word spread.

The project attracted considerable interest in the ecotourism industry for another reason as well. Part of the trail plan was a thorough visitor survey which could produce valuable information about trail users and their economic impact.

Results from their first visitor survey have just been released confirming that the trail has been used and enjoyed by birders. The average age of users was found to be 60, with an even split between males and females. The trail users were well educated with an average of 17 years of education, and the vast majority (92 per cent) were of Anglo descent. Almost half were urban dwellers and 97 per cent had traveled from home in the last 12 months to view wildlife. Fifty-two per cent saw themselves as active birders, 20 per cent were committed birders and 28 per cent were casual birders. On average they have been birding 20 years and spend an average of 13.1 days birding outside their state and 4.9 days birding outside of the U.S.

More than 90 per cent of the users listed being outdoors and the enjoyment of the sights, sounds and smells of nature as reasons for wildlife viewing. Fifty-four per cent found out about the trail through magazines, 39 per cent from birding organizations, 38 per cent from nature festivals and 28 per cent from friends. Most (68 per cent) travel with a spouse and on average spent $684 during their visit to the trail. Of that, $175 was spent on transportation, $212 on lodging, $180 on food, $57 on retail and $60 on other items. This translates to $78.52 per person per day for expenditures, slightly less than found in other surveys but trail users definitely shed the granola-eating, backpacking image.

So why is everyone so interested in birdwatching tourists?
·   They stay in hotels overnight
·   They almost always use restaurants (need coffee and have no time to cook)
·   They use airplanes and need gas for their rental cars
·   They buy expensive binoculars
·   They usually target bookstores for guides and references
·   They purchase mementos of their journeys.

From: Avitourism in Texas, prepared by Fermata, Inc. and John R. Stoll for Texas Parks and Wildlife Department, 1999.

Reprinted from: Ecotourism Management, Kalahari Management Inc., Spring 2000

The studies of special-interest travelers [35] and the British Columbia and Alberta market assessment [36] found that most people travel as a couple. A Canadian survey found that adventure travelers are more inclined to travel with friends or as part of a leisure group [37] while Americans pursuing soft adventure were most likely to travel with their spouse[38].

TRAVEL MOTIVATORS - There are many motivators behind travel, a particular activity or destination such as the desire to hike the West Coast Trail, or the need to take a break from a stressful job or escape a cold winter. Motivators for Canadian ecotourists from research done by J.A. Kretchman and P. Eagles were: wilderness, national parks and lakes, streams and mountains, and viewing flora and fauna; meeting new people; and experiencing new lifestyles. These are quite different from conventional travelers who reported visiting friends and relatives, shopping, nightlife and entertainment, amusement and theme parks, resort areas, and being together as a family as important motivators [30].

The ecotourism market assessment done for Alberta and British Columbia found trip motivators were scenery and new experiences. Experienced ecotourism travelers showed preference for outdoor activities while general consumers interested in ecotourism trips showed interest in culture-related activities, rest/relaxation, and family/friends [40].

The Travel Industry of America found that for many soft adventure travelers (48%), their interest in a specific adventure activity prompted the trip, however for a large number (29%), the adventure activity was the secondary reason for the trip[41]. Visit Florida's survey found that visiting parks (natural not theme) was the most popular activity for their visitors (see Figure 1-4) [42].

The study of special-interest travel buyers by Sorenson & Cresson found them looking for the chance to experience pre-planned activities they would not attempt on their own [43]. The World Wildlife Fund airport survey found sightseeing and natural history the highest reasons for selecting a destination country [44]. The Tourism Canada survey of adventure travelers found Canadian travelers like adventure, parks, and ethnic culture. International travel motivators varied by origin: British vacationers seek adventure, Germans are attracted by scenery and physical activities, French travelers seek adventure and excitement, and Japanese like wildlife viewing and outdoor activities [45].

The motivators common to many studies are seeing outstanding scenery and participating in the outdoors. Participation may be active, such as hiking, skiing, or water sports, or it may be passive, such as watching wildlife or experiencing another culture.

Creating a unique experience in one of these areas will distinguish your business from the competition. With higher incomes and education, ecotourists want a special incentive to chose your package over others. If you can provide access to unique or remote areas, or superior service through interpretation, that can be the edge that gets you the booking.

FIGURE 1-4 - **NATURE TOURISM GOING MAINSTREAM**

A recent nature-based tourism survey by Visit Florida, a public-private marketing partnership, produced some notable surprises. The survey on nature-based activities and the Florida Tourist showed some consistencies with previous ecotourism studies (such as trip preferences;) but there was some surprising information, notably regarding age and income of the nature-loving travelers.

People who engage in nature-based activities have a higher incidence of use of accommodation than people going to theme parks.

The survey showed a large proportion (51.6 per cent) of visitors to Florida included some type of nature-based activity (defined as hiking, biking, wildlife viewing, canoeing and going to parks) giving rise to the premise that this is no longer a niche market, but is in fact mainstream tourism.

The nature tourists tended to be younger than those not participating in nature based activity, with 24.9 to 26 per cent coming from the 25 to 34 age group and 30.5 to 36.5 per cent coming from the 35 to 49 age groups. As well, the correlation to household income was not as strong as was expected, i.e. nature tourists did not show a significantly higher household income than others. A possible explanation for that is the wide range of cost of entry for a variety of nature tourism activities.

Most Popular Nature-Based Activities for Vacationers in Florida	
Activity	**Per cent of Visitors Undertaking**
Visiting Parks	61.3 per cent
Wildlife viewing (non birds)	48.4 per cent
Hiking	36.6 per cent
Biking	21.5 per cent
Bird watching	20.4 per cent
Canoeing or kayaking	6.5 per cent

As expected, visiting parks was extremely important to nature-based activity enthusiasts (see table). Although no research was done into whether visitors have increased their awareness or contribution in conservation issues, Kerri Post of Visit Florida feels that the "best hope for preservation is visitation." With numbers like these there is no doubt the market exists for nature experiences, the question still to be answered is whether this level of demand can be met without compromising the wildlife or the visitor experience.

For information on this survey you can contact Kerri Post of Visit Florida at 850-488-5607 or visit their website at: www.flausa.com .

Reprinted from: Ecotourism Management, Kalahari Management Inc., Winter 2000

ECOTOURISM CHALLENGES

The ecotourism ethic requires adherence to stringent environmental standards.

Understanding the nature of ecotourism and the travelers who purchase ecotourism products is the first step in establishing an ecotourism business. As you will quickly discover, operators of ecotourism and nature tourism businesses face unique challenges.

The ecotourism ethic requires adherence to stringent environmental standards. Ecotourism has been used by some operators as a green-marketing strategy for a soft adventure product, while giving little consideration to operating practices or impacts on the environment and local communities. Operating in an environmentally-responsible manner requires additional planning and may increase start-up costs. Environmental impact assessments may be required, depending upon the nature of the business and its location.

Marketing an ecotourism product differs from that of conventional tourism products. The needs of ecotourists are greater in the areas of interpretation, variety and quality of experience, and group size. The ability to customize tours and access remote or hard-to-reach destinations are important factors.

Some market segments may be hard to reach. Avitourists are a fairly cohesive group. Many belong to at least one birding organization and can be accessed by advertising through birding organizations or birding magazines. Wildlife viewers and other natural history enthusiasts are more fragmented and require a broader selection of advertising tools.

Daily operations also present special difficulties. Maintaining the highly trained and diverse workforce requires sound human resource management. In North America, the tourism industry is very seasonal, with most activity occurring during summer months. Cash flow management to ensure the business survives the annual cycle is critical. The ecotourism product may need several operating seasons to generate a return to investors. This requires careful consideration in budgeting, start-up costs, and selection of financing.

These challenges and others are explored in the following chapters along with practical suggestions on ways to succeed and prosper as an ecotourism business owner.

KEY POINTS

· Ecotourism is the fastest growing segment of the tourism industry.
· Problems in defining ecotourism lead to confusion and difficulty in obtaining market research information.
· Ecotourism products take many forms. A wide range of services or facilities based on nature or culture may be marketed as ecotourism.

· Ecotourists are well-educated travelers requiring access to a variety of activities and unique destinations.

· Ecotourism ventures have much in common with conventional tourism operations but face special challenges in the areas of marketing, planning, and operations. A demanding client base, a high level of commitment to conservation, and often, the need to operate in remote locations, require extra effort.

WORKS CITED

1 The Ecotourism Society, "The Ecotourism Society Fact Sheet Collection," North Bennington, VT.

2 W. Whitlock, K. Romer, and R.H. Van Becker, *Nature Based Tourism: An Annotated Bibliography*, Clemson, South Carolina, USA, Strom Thurmond Institute, 1991.

3 Tourism Canada, *Adventure Travel in Canada: An Overview of Product, Market and Business Potential*, February 1995.

4 Canadian Heritage, Industry Canada, British Columbia Ministry of Small Business, Tourism and Culture, Alberta Economic Development and Tourism, and Outdoor Recreation Council of British Columbia, *Ecotourism- Nature/Adventure/Culture: Alberta and British Columbia Market Demand Assessment,* December 1994, p. 1.

5 Kreg Lindberg and Donald Hawkins, ed., *Ecotourism: A Guide For Planners and Managers,* The Ecotourism Society, 1993, p. 12.

6 Somerset, R. Waters, *Travel Industry World Yearbook The Big Picture - 1995 - 1996,* Child and Waters Inc., Rye, New York, 1996.

7 Canadian Heritage, Industry Canada, British Columbia Ministry of Small Business, Tourism and Culture, Alberta Economic Development and Tourism, Outdoor Recreation Council of British Columbia, *Ecotourism- Nature/Adventure/Culture: Alberta and British Columbia Market Demand Assessment*, December 1994, p. ES-1.

8 World Tourism Organization, *2001 National Survey of Fishing, Hunting, and Wildlife Associated Recreation*, U.S. Government Printing Office, Washington, D.C.

9 World Tourism Organization, *Torism 2020 Vision*.

10 Tourism Canada, *Adventure Travel in Canada: An Overview*, March 1995, p. 5.

11 The Ecotourism Society, "The Ecotourism Society Fact Sheet Collection," North Bennington, VT.

12 Canadian Heritage, Industry Canada, British Columbia Ministry of Small Business, Tourism and Culture, Alberta Economic Development and Tourism, Outdoor Recreation Council of British Columbia, *Ecotourism- Nature/Adventure/Culture: Alberta and British Columbia Market Demand Assessment*, December 1994.

13 Lynne Sorensen and Dave Cresson, *Market Research Special Interest Travel Buyers*, Consumer Survey Center, Inc., 1992.

14 Ro Wauer, "Profile of an ABA Birder," *Birding*, June 1991.

15 Texas Parks and Wildlife Department, *Avitourism in Texas*, 1999.

16 VISIT FLORIDA, *Nature-Based Activities and the Florida Tourist*, May 1999.

17 Travel Industry Association of America, *The Adventure Travel Report, 1997*,1997.

18 Texas Parks and Wildlife Department, *Avitourism in Texas*, 1999.

19 Travel Industry Association of America, *The Adventure Travel Report, 1997*,1997.

20 Ro Wauer, "Profile of an ABA Birder," *Birding*, June 1991.

21 David A. Fennell and Bryan J. A. Smale, "Ecotourism and Natural Resource Protection,"

Tourism Recreation Research, Vol. 17 (1), 1992, pp. 21-32.

22 James R. Butler, Glen T. Hvenegaard, and Doug K. Krystofiak, *Economic Values of Bird-Watching at Point Pelee National Park,* Canada.

23 VISIT FLORIDA, *Nature-Based Activities and the Florida Tourist*, May 1999.

24 Canadian Heritage, Industry Canada, British Columbia Ministry of Small Business, Tourism and Culture, Alberta Economic Development and Tourism, Outdoor Recreation Council of British Columbia, *Ecotourism-Nature/Adventure/Culture: Alberta and British Columbia Market Demand Assessment*, December 1994.

25 Ro Wauer, "Profile of an ABA Birder," *Birding*, June 1991.

26 Texas Parks and Wildlife Department, *Avitourism in Texas*, 1999.

27 David A. Fennell and Bryan J. A. Smale, "Ecotourism and Natural Resource Protection," *Tourism Recreation Research,* Vol. 17 (1), 1992, pp. 21-32.

28 Travel Industry Association of America, *The Adventure Travel Report, 1997*,1997.

29 Elizabeth Boo, *Ecotourism: The Potentials and Pitfalls*, World Wildlife Fund, Washington, D.C., 1990.

30 U.S. Department of the Interior, Fish and Wildlife Service and U.S. Department of Commerce, Bureau of the Census, *2001 National Survey of Fishing, Hunting, and Wildlife Associated Recreation*, U.S. Government Printing Office, Washington, D.C.

31 Tourism Canada, *Adventure Travel in Canada: An Overview of Product, Market and Business Potential,* February 1995.

32 James R. Butler, Glen T. Hvenegaard, and Doug K. Krystofiak, *Economic Values of Bird-Watching at Point Pelee National Park,* Canada.

33 The Ecotourism Society, "The Ecotourism Society Fact Sheet Collection," North Bennington, VT.

34 Elizabeth Boo, *Ecotourism: The Potentials and Pitfalls*, World Wildlife Fund, Washington, D.C., 1990.

35 Lynne Sorensen and Dave Cresson, *Market Research Special Interest Travel Buyers*, Consumer Survey Center, Inc., 1992.

36 Canadian Heritage, Industry Canada, British Columbia Ministry of Small Business, Tourism and Culture, Alberta Economic Development and Tourism, Outdoor Recreation Council of British Columbia, *Ecotourism- Nature/Adventure/Culture: Alberta and British Columbia Market Demand Assessment*, December 1994.

37 Tourism Canada, *Adventure Travel in Canada: An Overview of Product, Market and Business Potential,* February 1995.

38 Travel Industry Association of America, *The Adventure Travel Report, 1997*,1997.

39 J. A. Kretchman and P. Eagles, "An Analysis Of The Motives Of Ecotourists In Comparison To The General Canadian Population," *Loisir et Societe,* 1990, Vol. 13 (2), pp. 499 508.

40 Canadian Heritage, Industry Canada, British Columbia Ministry of Small Business, Tourism and Culture, Alberta Economic Development and Tourism, Outdoor Recreation Council of British Columbia, *Ecotourism- Nature/Adventure/Culture: Alberta and British Columbia Market Demand Assessment*, December 1994.

41 Travel Industry Association of America, *The Adventure Travel Report, 1997*,1997.

42 VISIT FLORIDA, *Nature-Based Activities and the Florida Tourist*, May 1999.

43 Lynne Sorensen and Dave Cresson, *Market Research Special Interest Travel Buyers*, Consumer Survey Center, Inc., 1992.

44 Elizabeth Boo, *Ecotourism: The Potentials and Pitfalls*, World Wildlife Fund, Washington, D.C., 1990.

45 Tourism Canada, *Adventure Travel in Canada: An Overview,* March 1995.

2 THE PLANNING PROCESS

STRATEGIC PLANNING: DEVELOPING YOUR BUSINESS

You may think strategic planning does not apply to you ecotourism business. "My business is too small for strategic planning." "This is just a bunch of theoretical planning with no real use." Well you are wrong! The planning process, whereby you consider what your business can do and where it is likely to be successful, is essential to your business future. Planning will lay the groundwork for your marketing efforts but most importantly, it will help you make the go/no-go decision on your venture.

Planning can work even better if applied on a community level. There are more stakeholders to help identify possible negative impacts in time to mitigate them. They can also identify other ecotourism or related business opportunities to help build community support and enthusiasm.

In its simplest form, a good plan identifies the opportunities, outlines ways to capitalize on these opportunities, and develops an implementation strategy for the most viable alternatives. Sometimes referred to as strategic planning, it is as basic as determining what your business will be, what products you will offer, and to whom you will sell your products. The process is outlined in Figure 2-1. The planning steps are discussed below.

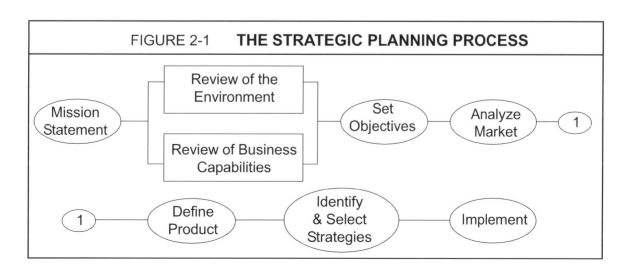

FIGURE 2-1 THE STRATEGIC PLANNING PROCESS

MISSION STATEMENT

Your mission statement tells the world (and yourself) the essence of your business. It conveys why your business exists, and in some cases, your vision of the future. It can be one sentence, it can be several, but it should include what you do, how you do it, who your customers are, and why you do what you do.

An example of a mission statement is "Green Ecotours provides outstanding natural history trips for domestic and international travelers. We use expert guides and visit undiscovered destinations to impart a sense of stewardship for the environment." This mission statement tells:

Mission statements tell the world why your business exists and your vision of the future.

- · What they do - provide outstanding natural history trips
- · How they do it - by using expert guides and visiting undiscovered destinations
- · Who their target customers are - domestic and international travelers
- · Why they do what they do - to impart a sense of stewardship for the environment

Compare your mission statement to these criteria. Does it give you a clear understanding of your business? Will it give other people a clear idea of your business?

Once you start to consider your options, you may feel yourself pulled in many different directions. You may have planned on doing back-country ski trips for overseas visitors but you have been approached for adventure trips to South America for outbound travelers. Evaluating opportunities and focusing on alternatives will be much easier if you start with a clear idea of where you are going and what you value.

EXTERNAL REVIEW OF THE ENVIRONMENT

An important step in the planning process is to assess the physical, economic, and political setting in which you operate. This will help you define the products you can offer.

As a potential tour operator in rural Wisconsin, you may be unaware of regional attractions or may downplay the area's ability to attract tourists. Completing a review of the physical ecology as part of a resource inventory will make you aware of a range of environmental settings in your area.

RESOURCE INVENTORY - A resource inventory as the name suggest, is an inventory of things in your community or operating area that can be used in developing an ecotourism product. You will want to consider:

- · Natural or scenic attractions
- · Historical attractions

· Cultural or social attractions

· Accommodations

· Restaurants

· Interpretive services

· Transportation

· Infrastructure

· Human resources

Use the resource inventory form featured in Figure 2-2 to do an analysis of your product, market, and geographic area. When completing the resource inventory, be sure to assess what attractions and facilities exist, the quality of each, and where improvements are needed. This may help you identify or expand your market niche.

The area you consider for the inventory could be small (your town or county), or it could be a much larger region or a grouping of several regions. If you are going to specialize in sea kayaking trips, you may be considering resources in Canada, the United States, Mexico, and beyond.

For small businesses with limited funds and manpower, it may be sufficient to re-view only the area where you will operate. A bike rental company wanting to add ecotouring to its customer services would likely start by identifying points of interest within a few hours cycling time. Existing guidebooks, chamber of commerce directo-ries and publications, resource managers, and experienced local cyclists would all be good sources of information.

ASSESSING GOVERNMENT REGULATIONS - Government serves many important roles. It protects common environments for the use of all people and sets minimum standards for the operation of business. Government directs individual and business activities through legislation and through rules, codes, and ordinances. Being familiar with regulatory requirements is extremely important for ecotourism businesses.

If your business involves the construction of a major facility, you will likely be subject to environmental impact assessment (EIA). If you only plan to conduct tours you may be relieved of many EIA requirements; however, you will always want to review impacts of any proposed activity to prevent harm to the physical ecology or local culture. Your business will likely be required to have a business license and may need to meet requirements for technical skills, first aid, and area knowledge.

First, determine the regulatory requirements for your area. Contact the agencies that may have jurisdiction in the area in which you plan to operate. Often this involves federal, state/provincial, and municipal governments. You may also cross functional boundaries and find you are dealing with planning, tourism, environment, and fish and wildlife

FIGURE 2-2   RESOURCE INVENTORY

Resource	Exists or Number	Unique Features	Product Quality	Future Potential: Low Medium High	Descriptions/ Problems
Natural or Scenic Attractions					
beaches			L	L	Cold, algae bloom
bird species		300 species	H	H	
birdwatching sites			L	M	Poor parking
canyons					
caves					
cliffs					
climate					
deserts		Hot, dry			
fishing			M	H	Good fly fishing
forests			H	H	Logging conflicts
fungus					
geological formations		Hoodoos	M	L	No public crimes
hiking trails		Uncrowded	M	M	Maps not distributed
islands					
lakes					
lichen		Vast wetlands	M	H	Low local awareness of potential
mammals					
mountains			H	H	Funding needed
nature trails		See two ranges	H	H	Multiple use conflicts
parks and protected areas				M	
plants			M	H	
rivers		Class 3 rapids	H	H	
waterfalls			M	M	
wilderness			L	L	Few, hard to access
other			M – H	H	
Historical Attractions					
indigenous sites					
interpretive centers					More work needed
museums				M	
other			L	L	
Cultural and Social Attractions					
festivals					
special events			M – H	H	Major birding festivals
traditional lifestyles			M	K	Community orientated
other					
Accommodation					
bed and breakfasts					
campgrounds		Great views	M	M	Off beaten path
hostels			M – H	M – H	Limited RV sites
hotels					
inns					
lodges			M	M	
motels			L	M	Upgrading required
other					

Restaurants					
casual					
ethnic			L	M	Need more visitors
fine dining			L	L	
health			H	H	
theme					
specialty					
other			M	M	
Interpretive Services					
bus tours					
dramatic presentations					
guided walks					
guiding services					
step-on services					
talks			M	H	Offered on some paddling trips
video			H	M	Provided by parks services, limited number
other					
Transportation					
airline service		Private aircraft only	L	L	150 miles to nearest commercial airport
animal transport (e.g.					
boat service		Hunting outfitters	M	L – M	traditional activity
bus service					
ferry service					
helicopter service		Rentals	M	M	
rail service					
other		Local tours	M	M	Need more interpretation
Infrastructure					
communication services		One internet café	H	H	
medical services		One regional hospital	M	M	
police services			M	M	Low crime/large area, slow response time
roadways			L – H	H	Able to reach all areas
sewage systems		Adequate for existing systems	M	M	
other					
Human Resources					
first-aid personnel					
guides					
hospitality workers					
marketing			H	H	
support staff			M	H	Need more
interpreters			L	H	Hard to find/ keep staff
other			M	H	Need more cooperative marketing programs

departments. This is an area where it pays to be thorough. You do not want to proceed with your plans to build a fly fishing lodge in a state park, only to find out that you have not complied with fishery legislation for the river or legislation for other states downstream of your camp.

Analysis of EIAs and government regulations help you assess both the feasibility and viability of your business venture.

You may find you cannot obtain approval for your idea or the cost of undertaking an EIA is too great. By identifying obstacles early, you may be able to alter the location or nature of your business to make it feasible. This is sometimes called fatal-flaw analysis, as it flushes out obstacles that if not overcome, would make it impossible to proceed.

Dealing with bureaucracies can be time consuming and costly. Be realistic in setting deadlines. If you are counting on getting approval to operate in an area within a few weeks or months and the process actually takes a year or two, you will need to plan for alternative cash flow sources and hold back your marketing efforts to avoid customer disappointment. The amount of time to obtain approvals varies with the scope of the ecotourism product and the extent of community support you have achieved. Talk to other operators early in the process; you may be surprised to find it can cost hundreds or thousands of dollars to deal with regulatory requirements, and you may need to reevaluate your plans.

As for ongoing operating permits, in the past, government may have been lax in enforcing requirements for licenses and permits. This is changing, as government looks for more opportunities to recover costs. In many national parks, license fees are increasing rapidly and the financial incentive to enforce compliance is growing.

It should be recognized that permits are not required for all activities. Activities that do not occur in protected spaces, or are of short duration and low risk, are situations where you may be allowed to operate without permits. While a business may not need a permit for a specific activity, a very similar activity in another jurisdiction, or an area with a different protection status, may require a permit.

Be watchful of new legislation that may require you to have a permit where none was required previously. You can provide input by attending hearings or talking with government and community representatives so that your business is not adversely affected by unrealistic regulation.

ANALYSIS OF YOUR COMPETITORS - Do not forget to evaluate your competitors. Understand what products they offer, who their customers are, and what their strengths and weaknesses are. Their strengths can guide you and their weaknesses may be areas of opportunity.

While there may be other companies offering canoeing trips, perhaps no one locally is offering trips with a historical slant. One company in Rocky Mountain House, Alberta,

Analysis of your competitors may provide insight into new opportunities for your business.

offers traditional voyageur canoe experiences and provides historical anecdotes as part of the trip. This has special appeal for those interested in history or culture and has generated interest from travel writers because it is unique.

Take time to identify both your direct and indirect competitors. An amusement park may not seem like a competitor, but if it is offering a leisure product to your potential clients, it is a competitor. Find out what price your competitors charge, their strategies for marketing and customer service, and any unique product characteristics they offer.

Understanding your competitors and how you can distinguish your product from theirs will become very important if you are seeking bank financing or investors. Often your bank manager or loan officer will not be an expert in tourism. If anything, they may know enough about tourism to feel it is a high-risk area. You will need to explain why you are different from other tourism businesses.

Many ecotourism businesses require a relatively small investment in equipment and working capital, an advantage when dealing with banks. On the other side, the small tangible asset base means that banks do not see much collateral on which to base a loan. Explaining how your business is different from others will demonstrate your ability to generate sales revenue and, ultimately, the cash flow to repay lenders.

INTERNAL REVIEW OF YOUR BUSINESS

The internal review of your business capability will define strengths and weaknesses. A strength is something your business possesses that provides a competitive advantage or helps it function better. Examples of strengths and weaknesses are shown in Table 2-1.

Many small operators find that a shortage of money is one of their weaknesses. On the strength side, they may have a strong knowledge of flora and fauna, or they may have exclusive guiding rights to a protected area. This can keep out competitors and help a small company become a recognized provider of unique trips.

Identify your weaknesses before your competition does. You can count on them to use your shortcomings to increase their sales. Once your business deficiencies are identified, do not ignore them for you can be putting your business at serious risk. Look for ways to turn weaknesses into strengths. If you are located a long distance from an international airport, you could overcome this weakness by offering charter flights as part of your package.

It is important to acknowledge operation weakness and outline plans to correct them. Savvy investors will be aware of your weak points, and a lack of acknowledgment and preparation could leave investors with the impression you are deceiving them or you have not thought through your entire operation. Neither of these is desirable!

SWOT Analysis - A tool that can be helpful in summarizing your analysis of the physical

A SWOT Analysis is a valuable tool that should be routinely used by all businesses.

and business setting and the abilities of your company, is the Strength-Weakness Opportunity-Threat (SWOT) analysis taught in many business courses. This is a concise summary accounting of the pluses and minuses of your business. You identify the strengths and the weaknesses of your business. Be honest! Opportunities and threats are usually external. Opportunities could be favorable economic conditions or removal of government restrictions on travel; threats could be closure of an area to travelers. An example of a SWOT analysis for an ecotourism business is shown in Table 2-1.

TABLE 2-1 **SWOT ANALYSIS - SOFT ADVENTURE TRAVEL COMPANY**	
Strengths · Access to full range of trained guides · Close to international airport · Permits to operate in 3 national parks · Partnership with hotel company for cross promotion	**Opportunities** · No new permits are being offered in national parks, therefore existing ones will have greater value · Creation of several social clubs in neighboring cities provides a potential market · Currency fluctuations are attracting more international visitors · Research indicates baby boomers are looking for more active vacations
Weaknesses · Short of working capital · Lack of four season camping equipment · No Internet site	**Threats** · May not be able to access other national parks · Areas allowing mountain biking is shrinking

OBJECTIVE SETTING

Setting goals and objectives gives you targets to shoot for. They tell you how to recognize success when it arrives. Each person will pick a different way to measure their business performance. You will want to pick goals that are fairly broad, such as "to be the leading provider of sea kayaking trips, as measured by sales, to Baja California in five years."

To achieve your goals, establishing several smaller objectives will make the task easier. An objective should be specific, measurable wherever possible, and have a time frame for completion. Selling as many kayaking trips as possible is not a well-defined objective. If this was restated as "sell 15 kayak trips of 4 days duration for the spring of 2008," it would be a more meaningful objective.

If you want to be sure your objective is meaningful, ask yourself how you will know when you have reached your target. If you cannot describe what your success will look like, you need to rework your objectives.

ANALYZING THE MARKETPLACE

Although your business will ultimately succeed based on favorable financial results, reaching this point often depends on your success in market planning, which is covered in significant detail in Chapter 4. You must be able to analyze the potential ecotourism market and determine where you will have the best chance of success.

Gathering primary market research is often too expensive and time-consuming for individual businesses, so you may want to focus your efforts on reviewing secondary data. These could be studies done by tourist associations or governments. Many are not specific to ecotourism, but may be relevant to you. There will be more studies done in the area of ecotourism as interest increases.

A careful review of the marketplace will tell you who your customers are and the best way to reach them.

You may also decide to gather market information by asking your customers questions. Where are they from? How did they hear of you? Why did they select you? If you find, as many ecotourism tour operators do, your company was recommended by a friend, you may spend less money on marketing through directories and give more thought on ways to stay in touch with, and in the minds of, your past customers.

An inexpensive way to gather information on your market is to use universities and colleges in your area. Business and tourism studies departments are often looking for real-world projects to develop skills and knowledge. Projects may be supervised to varying extents by professors. While they may have somewhat of a theoretical bent, they can be very helpful, especially in conducting surveys or other labor intensive tasks.

As a result of your market analysis, you will identify those types of people or groups (market segments) who fit your ecotourism products. Market segments may be defined by: demographics, activities undertaken, reasons for travel, and demographic origin.

As seen in Table 2-2, a segment may also represent groups of companies or recreational clubs. One ecotour company in the Rocky Mountains targets other companies operating in wilderness areas as a market for its bear awareness seminars.

TABLE 2-2 **EXAMPLES OF MARKET SEGMENTS**		
Segment Description	**Serious Adventurer**	**Incentive Group**
Age	25 - 40	35 - 55
Origin	Germany	North America
Gender	Mainly male	60% M, 40% F
Reasons for travel	Physical challenge	Unique reward for high performers
Length of stay	5 - 7 days	1 - 2 days

Once you have identified who your customers are, you will know where to focus your marketing dollars for maximum return on investment.

If you have identified a group of associations, clubs, or corporations, it will affect your marketing strategies, as you often approach organizations differently than you would individuals. Social clubs, for example, may require personal sales calls versus leaving lure brochures in visitor information centers.

Knowing your market segments helps you focus marketing dollars to provide the best return on investment instead of adopting a "broad brush" approach where everyone who ever traveled is a potential customer. Every dollar spent on marketing should generate several times that amount in sales. Advertising and marketing that are not targeted may result in far fewer sales. Customer profile information presented in chapter 1 can get you started on market research.

Analyzing your market by segment will also help you understand the characteristics of ecotourists. Find out what types of activities and lengths of trips are preferred by your segments. How people choose a tour is important. If one of your market segments is people driving the Alaska Highway and stop in your community for a geological foray, they may only be interested in a short side trip of several hours duration. You would perhaps plan to target your advertising at brochures distributed through travel information centers on the highway and roads leading to it.

DEFINING YOUR PRODUCT

With an inventory of your area's resources and an analysis of the marketplace, you can begin to identify, one, the products you are able to offer and, two, the products that would realistically be purchased by ecotourists.

If you have identified an abundance of bird life as a natural asset, you may develop a birdwatching tour for casual birdwatchers.

Product definition should only occur after market research and analysis of external and internal environments are completed.

You would decide how long the trip would be and what activities, lodging, and meals you would include. The structure of your product would be determined by the markets you are targeting and the prices you are able to charge.

If your market research indicates that most casual birdwatchers travel as a couple, are interested in culture as well as nature, and are looking for a trip of three to four days duration, you could develop a trip visiting a number of bird-viewing sites and an aboriginal center or event. You could also develop a weekend getaway package of similar content for people with less time.

When developing your product, it can be helpful to map out the activities and services that would be part of your offering. Using Figure 2-3, lay out in detail the activities that would be provided to the ecotourist. Include specific accommodations and meals as well as activities and free time.

When you have defined your product, cost out the individual components to arrive at a suitable selling price. (Pricing is covered in detail under marketing planning in Chapter 4.) You will still want to estimate your costs and selling price so you can determine if your product is likely to be successful. You may need to modify your product or define a new one.

A REALITY CHECK

The process of assessing whether your ecotourism operation is feasible and viable can be painful because you may not always get the answers you want. However, honesty is required if you are to avoid losing your investment or that of your investors.

Feasibility refers to whether you can actually do all the things you need to do to establish your business.

IS IT FEASIBLE? - Feasibility refers to whether you can actually do all the things you need to do to establish your business. Can you secure financing and regulatory approval? If you want to establish a back-country lodge, your business feasibility will depend upon approvals and permits to build and to operate. Can you secure special technology? Applied technology may affect the feasibility of your lodge. Permit approval could be contingent upon developing a working waste disposal system in a harsh physical setting that meets regulatory standards.

Tourism businesses already in existence may have an advantage over new operators, especially when it comes to regulatory issues. Some national parks limit the number of guiding permits they issue. One ecotourism operator in western Canada was particularly frustrated because no new guide permits for overnight trips into a park were available. Operators holding existing permits had unique access to wilderness areas. This situation is disconcerting if you are a competitor but helpful if you are lucky enough to have the permit.

FIGURE 2-3 **PRODUCT DEVELOPMENT WORKSHEET**			
Schedule	**Item/Activity**	**Provider**	**Cost**
Day 1			
Breakfast			
Morning Activities			
Lunch			
Afternoon Activities	transport from airport	Joe's shuttle	$45.00
Dinner	casual dinner	Heidi's Bistro	$12.00
Evening Activities	orientation talk/slide show	Nancy	$9.00
Day 2			
Breakfast	provided with hotel room	Mountainview Lodge	$30.00
Morning Activities	kayaking	River Runners	$20.00
Lunch	on river	River Runners	$8.00
Afternoon Activities	white water rafting	River Runners	$20.00
Dinner	barbeque	Bar Cee Ranch	$15.00
Evening Activities	star gazing	Bar Cee Ranch	
Day 3			
Breakfast	provided with hotel room	Mountainview Lodge	$30.00
Morning Activities	mountain biking	Bikes For You	$25.00
Lunch	picnic (late lunch)	Tina's Deli	$8.00
Afternoon Activities	guided hike	Nancy	$9.00
Dinner	box snack	Tina's Deli	$7.00
Evening Activities	transfer to airport	Joes' Shuttle	$45.00
Total Cost			$283.00
10% Contingency			$28.30
Overhead			$85.00
Total Net Cost			$396.30

Viability refers to whether your business is capable of developing and growing.

Is it Viable? - If your business passes the feasibility test, you then need to determine if it is viable. Viability refers to whether your business is capable of developing and growing. At this point in the planning process, you should have some idea of the market you hope to capture. From the work on pricing, you should have some idea of the revenues you hope to realize.

By applying an estimate of costs, both capital and operating, you can begin to determine whether the business is viable. You may be able to generate enough revenue to cover operating costs but are unable to repay a loan or pay dividends to shareholders.

Another part of the decision-making process unique to ecotourism is determining product viability on environmental grounds. You may realize the need to take in a greater number of tours to an area than first anticipated in order to cover costs. A new product or modifications of an existing one, changing the locations or trip type, may be needed to operate a viable business without compromising environmental principles.

Take time early in the process to assess viability even if high-level estimates are used. Thousands of dollars can be spent in developing a business plan, and obtaining architectural drawings, operating approvals, and permits. It is far wiser to assess your chances of success sooner rather than later, when large sums of money may have been spent.

THE NEED FOR A BUSINESS PLAN

If your business concept passes the feasibility and viability tests, you will want to develop your idea further. A business plan can be an effective way of developing an action guide for your strategies. It shows step-by-step how you will start and then operate your successful business. It outlines your business activities, marketing plans, and financial forecasts for one to five years.

A business plan is a written statement of your goals and objectives, business strategy, and plans for carrying out the strategy.

A detailed business plan will identify potential problems you are likely to encounter and needed solutions. It is also a mechanism for communicating your vision and plans to employees, investors, and bankers. In fact, without it, you will not proceed past the preliminary stages with your banker.

A business plan should be updated yearly with your new marketing and operating strategies. Continued forecasting of sales and expenses will show if your ideas are viable. As many ecotourism businesses operate on small profit margins, forecasting can help keep you profitable.

If you are just starting an ecotourism venture, a business plan is even more critical. It will force you to look objectively at the resource needed to develop a tour or service; the laws, codes, and ordinances to deal with; and the size and characteristics of the market. By understanding more about the ecotourism industry and putting "numbers' to your idea, you will have a better idea of what you are getting into. Some people will find factors they had not originally anticipated. Because of the state of the economy, there may be very few travelers in their part of the world. May be the financing cost are higher than planned. Or, the current market price for the product does not cover the cost of operating in a remote location. It is better to know your business idea is not feasible at the planning stage than when dollars are spent. Information on preparing a business plan is provided in Chapter 11.

GETTING YOUR COMMUNITY INVOLVED

Getting your community involved in ecotourism may be one of the hardest, yet personally and professionally rewarding activities you encounter in your business development.

The planning process can be an excellent way to involve members of your community in developing ecotourism in your area. By doing so, you can identify a broad range of opportunities not just for yourself but for others as well. If you develop a tour company that does natural history hikes into remote areas, there could be opportunities for local artisans to make and sell crafts. If you are building an eco-lodge, you could purchase your supplies locally. This may encourage local farmers to grow additional or special crops to supply your needs. You can create employment opportunities for people skilled in interpretation or knowledgeable in local history, culture, or ecology. A group of ecotour companies can create opportunities for service companies who can offer guide training, booking services, or internet site development. Whatever the connection, involving your community will increase opportunities, and get more support for your product, prevent surprises for local residents, and lessen resistance.

Let your story be known. Do not be worried that you may generate competition by discussing your business plans. Other tour operators in your area can actually strengthen your position by providing greater choice for tourists and the capacity to handle additional numbers of clients.

If you look at shopping centers, this is the principle they work under. One store on its own will not attract as many customers as a group of stores. It becomes even more powerful when a theme is maintained by all.

This can also apply to your ecotourism product. The Town of Estes Park, Colorado, was searching for a new vision for promoting their town as a tourism destination. As wildlife was a very visible part of their community, it became the theme around which they planned their promotional activities.

The process started with a small step, a picture of local wildlife was used on a lure brochure for the area. Hoteliers formed the Estes Park Accommodation Associations Betterment Fund. A voluntary tax on rooms supports wildlife viewing and conservation activities. A guide with wildlife viewing tips was published and hotel staffs were trained to promote good wildlife viewing habits.

The community has seen a major increase in visitors, specifically to experience wildlife. Hotels are booked solid in October with tourists for the elk rutting season. Community volunteers are visible along key roads to answer questions and keep people from harming sensitive environments and themselves. This is a clear case of business and conservation organizations working together. From their partnership, they have a better product and better management of tourism impacts.

KEY POINTS

· Planning is essential for assessing the ecotourism potential for an area.
· A resource inventory is an important tool for determining ecotourism products.
· A strategic plan depends heavily upon good marketing research and a well-developed marketing plan (see Chapter 4).
· Careful market research helps tailor products to meet the needs of specific market segments.
· Community involvement early in the planning process increases your likelihood of success.
· Assess the feasibility and viability of your product.

3

THE ECO
IN ECOTOURISM

THE DEVELOPMENT PHASE

The hallmark of ecotourism is natural resource conservation, which means minimizing impacts on the social, cultural, and physical environments of the host country. Weaving this environmental thread through your ecotourism business is a main part of what distinguishes your product from traditional tourism.

To be considered a true ecotourism venture, you must become environmentally responsible in all your business practices.

Putting the "eco" in your tourism operation will require additional planning early, and monitoring and evaluation once you are operational.

It may create additional start-up and operating costs that make it difficult to compete with other companies that bypass strict environmental responsibility. However, if tourism is to be sustainable, there will be a time when all tourism operates with environmentally-friendly business practices.

HOW DOES MY BUSINESS IMPACT THE ENVIRONMENT? - Although ecotourism pioneers may have envisioned it as a way to promote both nature and their economic well-being without harming the environment, many people have since come to the conclusion that there are few activities, if any, that have no environmental impact. The realistic challenge now is to minimize negative impacts.

In some cases, there will be legislative requirements through such processes as an Environmental Impact Assessment (EIA) to monitor ecological impacts and mitigate harmful effects. More often, there are few legal requirements to tread softly and it is left to the ecotourism operator to determine what constitutes unacceptable impacts and how to operate in a responsible manner.

Start by checking with local, regional, and federal authorities to determine if and when an EIA is required. EIA or not, it is desirable to design your facility or operation to minimize impacts. If structures will be built, their location and form should match the environment and cause as little disturbance as possible. Operating methods should minimize harmful impacts. Communication strategies should be put in place for employees and clients so standards for environmental protection are maintained. Perhaps most importantly, determine how to monitor your impacts. Selecting several key criteria, such as trail erosion and the number of annual animal sightings in an area, and measuring changes in these elements, will quantify your operation's impact.

If you are subject to an EIA, this will be a more formal review to determine if your business or businesses (if planning is being done at a community level) will adversely impact the physical environment. Requirements for an EIA will differ among governments and should be investigated early. In a project with large impacts on the environment and host community, some governments will expect you to be proactive in assessing impacts and soliciting community input.

Careful planning and incorporation of "eco-friendly," energy-saving materials will help keep your business "green" and healthy.

IF YOU WILL BE BUILDING - The ways in which you weave "green" business practices into your operations are myriad. If you are constructing a facility from the ground up, you have greater control of materials used and can influence future day-to-day operations. Harmony Bay in the U.S. Virgin Islands is an excellent example of an ecotourism lodge built with environmental sustainability in mind. Water pipes were attached beneath walkways between cabins, minimizing utility construction on the forest. Buildings were placed so as to minimize disturbances to trees. Cabins were located to take advantage of prevailing shade and breezes, eliminating the need for air conditioning.

Operating from existing buildings may limit the environmental-friendly items you can add easily and may require additional capital investment to incorporate energy-saving mechanisms.

Operating systems such as utilities and sewage should be designed for sensitive environmental conditions. Often operators will need to be creative in the development of physical buildings and operating systems, as operating in remote locations, at high altitudes, or in harsh climates, creates unique problems that are not met by readily-available construction materials.

At high altitude, where weather is often cold, compost toilets will not work well enough to handle wastes from a small lodge. You may be forced to develop your own technology or adapt existing technology to situations where it is unproved. Often, unique solutions mean greater costs, no guarantees from manufacturers, or a lack of bureaucratic understanding.

Using local craftsmen and artisans in the construction of a facility will help match the structure to its physical and cultural environment and provide specific benefits to the community.

WHEN DEVELOPING TOURS - Select tour destinations and routes that will withstand ecotourism activities, and determine what level of activity is appropriate. An area where facilities already exist, such as pit latrines or hardened trails, can likely withstand more visitation than where no facilities exist. You may discard a destination or route because it cannot support the level of visitation to make your tour viable financially. Such environmental regard distinguishes good ecotourism organizations.

SETTING YOUR COMPANY'S ENVIRONMENTAL POLICIES

While many larger organizations develop policies, sometimes to excess, small or medium organizations may not feel developing policies is necessary. Policies are critical, however, for translating your vision and goals to your staff. Some areas of concern are:
- Tour Development: group size, number of trips to an environment, criteria for selecting a destination
- Tour Operation: camping practices, vehicle operation, food purchases, food preparation, waste disposal
- Human Resources: recruiting, training, remuneration
- Marketing: printing practices, cooperative marketing, community relations, donations, partnerships with conservation groups
- Administration: recycling, vendor selection

Writing down your policies will help define your business practices.

Environmental stewardship is manifested in many ways. Businesses may develop many different operating practices based upon the owners beliefs and pocketbook, market demands, environment characteristics, and legislation. Writing down your policies will help define your business practices.

Some owners have found they can not afford all of their environmental-friendly practices, at least not initially. This can cause tremendous stress as they must choose between personal values and business actions. In some way this is the biggest challenge for ecotourism businesses.

To balance making money with sustainable tourism practices, may require courage. When you must cancel a confirmed tour booking because a wildlife species at your destination is stressed from environmental conditions such as a bad winter and your presents will only increase the stress, you will have truly experienced the world of ecotourism!

Ultimate Adventures of Grande Prairie, Canada has demonstrated leadership in ecotourism by developing comprehensive policies for all areas of its business. Shutting off the vehicle engines while waiting, parking only in parking lots and not on vegetation along roadways, and not using disposable coffee cups while traveling are examples. These policies are helpful in communicating what good tourism practices look like to guides and other staff members.

SUSTAINING ENVIRONMENTAL POLICIES IN DAILY OPERATIONS

Many ecotourism businesses operate in protected areas such as national parks. Under these conditions, environmental standards are very high. Simply disposing of waste products and recycling can take time and money to plan and execute. A remote lodge cannot hook up to a local sewage system - you will have to create the local sewage system and ensure it meets requirements.

Waste products from kitchens present a challenge. National parks require garbage containers that are bear-proof. It is good environmental practice to dispose of all food wastes properly so wildlife behaviors are not altered nor people's lives jeopardized.

When greening your business review all the steps in the business cycle.

When greening your business review all the steps in the business cycle. Look at how you will market the product, deliver the ecotourism experience, monitor the business impacts, and administer the business. Each of these can be make more sustainable with extra planning.

An excellent example of the care that can be taken operating an ecotourism business is seen at the Harmony Bay Camp. Their operating guidelines outline sound environmental practices. An excerpt is shown in the case study on the following page. Offering happy hour prices only on drinks that come in bulk, such as draft beer and cask wine, is a simple yet effective way of minimizing the cost of shipping and the disposal of excess packaging. This helps educate tourists about ways to reduce their impact on the earth's resources.

When developing your operating procedures, look to organizations who have shown leadership in environmental responsibility. Many communities have conservation groups that promote the four Rs (reduce, reuse, recycle, and buy recycled) and can give or recommend literature to green your operation. Park service employees and your state department of natural resources will also provide information on standards. Utility companies can be helpful in suggesting ways to minimize energy usage.

Fairmont Hotels and Resorts developed *The Green Partnership Guide*, which has been the recipient of numerous awards. You can obtain information by contacting *Environmental Affairs, 100 Wellington Street West, Suite 1600, Toronto, Ontario, Canada M5K 1B7. The International Ecotourism Society,* at www.ecotourism.org also distributes a collection of operating codes for sustainable tourism.

CASE STUDY: ECOTOURISM AT MAHO BAY AND HARMONY STUDIOS

Impact on the Environment

Waste management is a major concern in our world today. An effective waste management program can make a difference in our relationship to the natural world. This not only includes management of garbage, but also reduction of wasted energy and water resources. There are four alternatives which can help to cut back on waste:

1. *Reduce* garbage and use of resources
2. *Reuse* items, energy and water resources
3. *Recycle* garbage and resources
4. *Buy recycled* products (to close the product life-cycle loop)

Reduction at Maho Bay

- Bulk purchasing for Kitchen and Housekeeping departments (e.g. condiments, cleaning and paper products)
- Large freezer and cooler allow plenty of room for bulk buying of perishables for the kitchen
- Instead of individual cereal boxes at breakfast, homemade granola is offered
- Cigarettes are not sold in the Store, and many "No Smoking" areas have been established
- Eliminated use of styrofoam food and beverage containers — There is no "take-out" at Maho Bay
- Drastically reduced the number of disposable bottles and cans by installing a draft beer and soda system at the Restaurant
- The Restaurant and Store consider packaging when ordering specific items — some products have been dropped due to excessive packaging
- Propane tanks supplying the stoves in tent-cottages are refillable
- Guests are provided with $2\frac{1}{2}$ gallon refillable drinking water dispensers
- The Restaurant and Store have consolidated ordering of supplies to reduce traffic and fuel consumption by delivery trucks
- Regular shuttles are arranged for guest transportation to cut down the need to rent cars
- Unlike most resorts, there is minimal use of motorized vehicles by Housekeeping to cover the distances between tent-cottages, Laundry and storage areas, or by Maintenance between garbage cans and garbage truck
- Low water-use toilets are utilized
- Spring-loaded faucets are installed in sinks and showers
- Running water is not supplied to most tent-cottages
- There are limited shower hours in bath houses
- All of these efforts have resulted in extremely low water usage: 25-30 gallons per person, about a third of the average per person water usage in the U.S.
- Temperature of coolers and freezers in the Store is constantly monitored

· Tent-cottage design and fabric capitalise on cooling trade winds and natural light

· Design also provides easy cleaning — surfaces are swept or wiped down, and no electrically-powered cleaning equipment is needed

· Construction amidst trees provides natural shade; electric fans used for cooling instead of air-conditioning

· As new tent-cottages are built, design improvements continue to be made for better ventilation, leading to lower energy consumption from electric fans.

· Thermal coolers are provided instead of electrically-powered refrigerators.

· Water in bath houses and laundry is not heated.

· Future plans include replacing light bulbs with halogen-type bulbs, and putting timers on electric switches in bath houses.

At Harmony, all eight units were built to use alternatives to traditional energy sources. Energy generated by solar panels is stored in batteries which provide all of the electricity for the units. Cisterns collect rainwater that is filtered and used. Waste water is treated and used for toilet-flushing and irrigation of shade-providing plants. The wind scoop design of the ceilings helps provide natural ventilation and the mirror glazing on the windows lessens the energy usage needed for cooling the units.

Source: Maho Bay Camps and Harmony Studios, *Ecotourism at Maho Bay*

ENVIRONMENTAL POLICIES FOR LOW-IMPACT OUTDOOR PRACTICES - Most ecotourism activities occur in the great outdoors. Many organizations have done excellent work in developing low-impact camping and hiking guidelines for outdoor recreationists that would allow future generations to enjoy our wild places. Provide this information to your clients. It will help ensure people traveling in wilderness settings are good environmental stewards and neighbors.

The internet is a good source of environmentally-responsible operating practices.

The internet is a good source of environmentally-responsible operating practices; several organizations provide considerable information on low-impact travel. Two such organizations are Princeton University and Leave No Trace, Inc. Internet addresses can change over time, so use web search engines to locate these sites and others. Excerpts from Leave No Trace, Inc. suggest:

· Plan ahead and prepare

· Concentrate impacts in high use areas

· Spread out use and impact in pristine areas

· Avoid places where impact is just beginning

· Pack it in, pack it out

· Properly dispose of what you cannot pack out

· Leave what you find

· Use fire responsibly

These principles apply in all situations. Additional practices for ecosystems such as mountains, deserts, and coastal regions are detailed in booklets such as *Pacific Northwest Skills and Ethics Booklet*,[1] or *Rocky Mountain Skills and Ethics Booklet*.[2]

Another good source of minimum-impact camping techniques is REI, a provider of outdoor gear in Seattle, Washington. Their guidelines [3] recommend, among other things:

· Suppress desire to shortcut switchbacks
· Take rest breaks on hardened areas to minimize impact
· Select shelter sites that have already been used to minimize camp expansion
· Where possible, position your tent so it blends into the environment
· Protect water sources from contamination
· Keep fires small or enjoy the experience of a fireless evening
· Speak softly, save rowdy games and songs for another time

Distributing pre-trip information to clients helps minimize negative impacts on the environment.

ENVIRONMENTAL POLICIES FOR CLIENT EDUCATION - One way an operator can help ensure their business does not have a negative impact on the environment is to educate their clients. A good way to do this is through pre-trip information. One tour operator who specializes in adventure travel to Asia and Africa provides several opportunities for trip participants to meet prior to the trip. Here, they can learn about the destinations ecology and culture. In addition to explaining what equipment and clothing is necessary for a safe and enjoyable nature experience, guides point out the unique features of the host community and sensitize travelers to their role. If people are told that they can gauge whether they are too close to an animal by noting changes in its behavior, they will have a better, safer experience.

We cannot expect people to be good ecotourists if we have not taken time to explain what is a good ecotourist. Some companies use a written code-of-ethics to explain what behavior they expect from ecotourists. This is a good start, although guides need to reinforce the concepts throughout the trip for maximum effect.

Inform your clients what it means to be a good ecotourist.

The American Society of Travel Agents (ASTA) Ten Commandments of Ecotourism are shown in Figure 3-1. These commandments are basic and useful for orienting people before they take an ecotour.

Another way to educate clients is to follow up with information after the tour. Having visited an area, people often develop a personal interest in the conservation issues that face a region and may look for opportunities to donate money, goods, or time. A group of North American ecotourists returning from Matusadona Park, Zimbabwe, gathered batteries and rechargers for a rhino-tracking project to preserve the remaining population of these rare animals. Providing information on area organizations can complete the travel experience and build partnerships with the host community.

FIGURE 3-1 **ASTA'S TEN COMMANDMENTS ON ECOTOURISM**

Whether on business or leisure travel:

1. **Respect the frailty of the earth.** Realize that unless all are willing to help in its preservation, unique and beautiful destinations may not be here for future generations to enjoy.

2. **Leave only footprints. Take only photographs.** No graffiti! Do not take away "souvenirs" from historical sites and natural areas.

3. To make your travels more meaningful, **educate yourself about the geography, customs, manners and cultures of the region you visit.** Take time to listen to the people. Encourage local conservation efforts.

4. **Respect the privacy and dignity of others.** Inquire before photographing people.

5. **Do not buy products made from endangered plants or animals**, such as ivory, tortoise shell, animal skins and feathers. Read "Know Before You Go," the U.S. Customs list of products which cannot be imported.

6. **Always follow designated trails.** Do not disturb animals, plants or their natural habitats.

7. Learn about and **support conservation-oriented programs and organizations** working to preserve the environment.

8. Whenever possible, **walk or utilize environmentally-sound methods of transportation.** Encourage drivers of public vehicles to stop engines when parked.

9. **Patronize those** (hotels, airlines, resorts, cruise lines, tour operators and suppliers) who advance energy and environmental conservation; water and air quality; recycling; safe management of waste and toxic materials; noise abatement; community involvement; and which provide experienced, well-trained staff **dedicated to strong principles of conservation.**

10. Ask your ASTA travel agent to **identify those organizations which subscribe to ASTA Environmental Guidelines for air, land and sea travel.** ASTA has recommended that these organizations adopt their own environmental codes to cover special sites and ecosystems.

Source: *ASTA*

ASSESSING IMPACTS

One of the areas you must give consideration is your impact on the host community. It can be difficult to measure changes to physical and cultural environments. To determine if you have met your objectives, you must determine in advance which performance indicators relate to your business.

Although carrying capacity is often discussed, this concept becomes difficult to apply in the real world. Carrying capacity attempts to determine how many people an area can support before negative environmental impacts occur. In a complex ecosystem, determining this number can be very difficult, at best. Information, baseline or other, on species and ecosystems may be incomplete. It may often be difficult to isolate the causes of environment impacts.

Carrying capacity is giving way to Limits of Acceptable Change (LAC). Instead of determining the number of people that can visit an area, LAC represents the setting of limits where an increase in visitation would indicate an unacceptable environmental decline.

It is necessary to examine the cumulative impact of all businesses in an area.

It can be frustrating to realize there is a shortage of baseline information from which to set limits of acceptable change. If you do not know how many bears live in an area when you start operations, how can you accurately know if increasing the number of tours to an area has had a negative impact? An individual operator will also recognize that determining indicators of acceptable change may require a community or regional effort.

It is necessary to examine the cumulative impact of all businesses in an area. Isolating impacts from tourism may be difficult but necessary. Selecting indicators that relate only to tourism impacts, such as trail condition or number of back country permits issued, help to determine what level and type of tourism is occurring and by using these, provide comparisons to overall environmental change in the community. Non-tourism impacts may be isolated to some extent.

BUSINESS EVALUATION - On a micro level, an organization can evaluate its own business policies and practices to see if it is green and sustainable. An assessment is shown in Figure 3-2. If you rate high in all areas, pat yourself on the back. Continue to look for ways to improve, as time waits for no one and your competitors and clients will search for even more improvements. Where there is room for improvement, include that in your business plan for the next year.

FIGURE 3-2   **BUSINESS EVALUATION CRITERIA**

1 = No effort has been made to meet criteria
2 = Initial efforts made to meet criteria
3 = Some effort made to meet criteria, room still for improvement
4 = Good effort made to meet criteria, fine tuning required
5 = Have met criteria

1. The design and construction of your facility reflects the natural surroundings and culture of the area. 1 2 3 4 5 n/a

2. Renewable building materials were used in the construction of your facilities. 1 2 3 4 5 n/a

3. Guest areas are furnished with locally produced furniture and artwork. 1 2 3 4 5 n/a

4. You set a maximum number of clients that is compatible with the environmental sensitivity of the area. 1 2 3 4 5 n/a

5. You have a written environmental policy. 1 2 3 4 5 n/a

6. You have a code of conduct for your employees. 1 2 3 4 5 n/a

7. You have a code of conduct for travellers. 1 2 3 4 5 n/a

8. You pre-qualify clients. 1 2 3 4 5 n/a

9. You provide pre-trip information to your customers on the specific ecosystems and cultures visited. 1 2 3 4 5 n/a

10. You educate your clients about local and international laws regarding threatened plants and animals. 1 2 3 4 5 n/a

11. You prepare customers to buy and trade local products while respecting the indigenous culture. 1 2 3 4 5 n/a

12. You check water consumption and use regulating equipment on faucets and showers. 1 2 3 4 5 n/a

13. You take an active role in environmental or conservation organizations. 1 2 3 4 5 n/a

14. You make donations to environmental or conservation groups. 1 2 3 4 5 n/a

15. Your guides are local guides or your guides work with local guides. 1 2 3 4 5 n/a

16. Local people are represented in all levels of your operations.	1	2	3	4	5	n/a
17. You provide frequent training for your staff (i.e. at least seasonally).	1	2	3	4	5	n/a
18. You purchase food locally for your operations.	1	2	3	4	5	n/a
19. You promote the sale of local arts and handicrafts.	1	2	3	4	5	n/a
20. You encourage customers to stay on pathways.	1	2	3	4	5	n/a
21. Public or group transportation for your clients is encouraged.	1	2	3	4	5	n/a
22. You use gray waste water for watering and toilet rinsing.	1	2	3	4	5	n/a
23. You use environmentally friendly soaps.	1	2	3	4	5	n/a
24. You have undertaken an energy audit.	1	2	3	4	5	n/a
25. You use equipment to regulate lighting and heating.	1	2	3	4	5	n/a
26. You use energy saving electrical appliances, light bulbs, etc.	1	2	3	4	5	n/a
27. You have a recycling program.	1	2	3	4	5	n/a
28. You compost solid food waste.	1	2	3	4	5	n/a
29. You donate leftover food and outdated bedding to local non-profit organizations.	1	2	3	4	5	n/a
30. You use recycled paper and paper products.	1	2	3	4	5	n/a
31. You purchase in bulk where possible.	1	2	3	4	5	n/a
32. You avoid the use of disposable dishes, toilet articles, etc.	1	2	3	4	5	n/a
33. You provide beverages served in recyclable containers.	1	2	3	4	5	n/a
34. You remove waste from natural areas.	1	2	3	4	5	n/a
35. You give preference to equipment which has a long life and which can be repaired.	1	2	3	4	5	n/a
36. Your organization participates in a certification program for environmental commitment.	1	2	3	4	5	n/a

TOTAL SCORE

Source: *Kalahari Management Inc.* 1996

KEY POINTS

- Ecotourism requires strict adherence to environmentally-friendly business practices.
- Facilities should be designed to take advantage of local conditions and to minimize the physical, social, and cultural impact on the host environment.
- Developing environmental policies can be helpful in maintaining ecological integrity and in ensuring quality service throughout the organization.
- Operating in remote and sensitive settings requires adoption of low-impact methods.
- Functioning in remote sites often means additional costs and can present difficulties in obtaining equipment and supplies.
- Client education is critical to adapt the ecotourist to the place visited, as opposed to having the place adapt to the ecotourist.
- Going "green" is not only good for the environment but gives you an edge in marketing your product.

WORKS CITED

1 National Outdoor Leadership School, *Pacific Northwest Skills and Ethics Booklet,* 1995.

2 National Outdoor Leadership School, *Rocky Mountain Skills and Ethics Booklet,* 1994.

3 REI, Techniques *for the new wilderness ethic,* Seattle, Washington.

4 MARKETING YOUR PRODUCT

MARKETING VERSUS SELLING

Once you have developed an ecotourism product, you are faced with the reality of selling it. While you may have a ecotour product with lots of nature encounters and great customer service, you cannot sit back and wait for customers to arrive. For one thing they may not have heard of your town nor be aware of the attractions you offer. A good marketing plan will get your product in front of customers and convince them to book a trip.

For people without a marketing background, the whole area of sales and marketing can be intimidating. As a ecotourism owner, you must be involved to some extent in the marketing process, but that does not mean you have to become a professional salesperson.

Marketing defines potential buyers, their needs, and the best way to meet those needs.

First, you need to distinguish between selling and marketing. Marketing is the process by which you determine the potential buyers of your product, what their needs are, and how you can respond to those needs in a way that will encourage them to visit your business. It is a critical component and requires looking at the "big picture." Selling and promotional activities are part of marketing and occur when you contact people to persuade them to buy.

If selling does not sound appealing, you may be able to contract out that function at some point, but it is unlikely you will ever remove yourself totally from sales. After all, who is better equipped to convey the uniqueness and attractiveness of your tour or destination than the visionary who created the company and the product?

As you get involved in marketing you will realize it is a series of interconnected steps. You will identify potential customers and products to offer them. As you refine your ideas, you will determine how to reach customers at a reasonable cost. This leads to forecasts of sales levels, which will drive your budget process and related financial decisions. The following sections will take you through the process of developing a marketing plan.

DEVELOPING A MARKETING PLAN

Your marketing plan can build on the work already done for your strategic or long-term business plan. As you saw in Chapter 2, the strategic plan includes a market analysis and the matching of products with specific markets. You will be more successful by setting specific marketing objectives and developing strategies and activities to sell your product. The marketing plan allows you to budget for marketing activities and to evaluate the effectiveness of those activities. A good marketing plan has the following elements:

- Business objectives
- Situation analysis
- Market analysis
- Competitive analysis
- Product-market match
- Marketing objectives
- Positioning
- Marketing strategies
- Marketing activities

These components are explained in more detail below and should be followed in order. An overview of the process is shown in Figure 4-1.

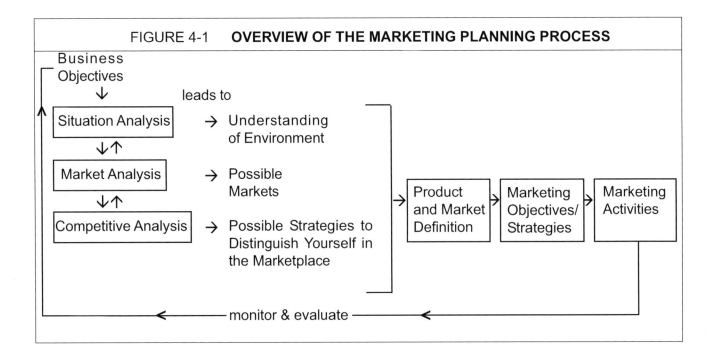

FIGURE 4-1   **OVERVIEW OF THE MARKETING PLANNING PROCESS**

BUSINESS OBJECTIVES - With any marketing plan, you need to know what you are trying to accomplish. Just wanting to sell more "stuff" is not specific enough to develop a good marketing plan. If you have a mission statement, refer to it. What is your business about? Who are your main customers? How do you want to accomplish your goals? If your mission statement calls for you to provide visitors with lifetime memories through experiences in nature, you will market your tours much differently than if you provide hiking and mountaineering activities for the adventure-minded traveller.

If you have a mission statement, use it.

Objectives developed in your strategic planning will also give you added direction. If one of your objectives is to generate a net profit of five percent, you will need to focus your marketing activities on tours that have a healthy profit margin. You may also need to look at a more upscale market that will pay a higher price for your product.

As you proceed through the steps of the marketing plan, you will be confronted with many alternatives. Refer to your mission statement and high-level objectives. You will find it easier to select options that generate profits while maintaining your commitment to the environment and host communities.

Part of situation analysis involves considering the negative influences along with the possitive.

SITUATION ANALYSIS - If you have completed a strategic plan, you have completed part of the situation analysis by taking an inventory of local tourism resources (see Chapter 2). If you did not undertake a strategic plan or some time has elapsed since you did a resource inventory, it is a good idea to update your inventory. Has a new orchid species been discovered in your region? Have new roads been built or an existing one closed, allowing more or less access to remote areas? Is there a new festival in your community with a cultural or nature component? This step will ensure you are familiar with the natural, cultural, and man-made features your business or community can use to meet the ecotourist needs.

You also want to consider any negative influences that have arisen in your area lately. Has a limit has been placed on the number of tours on a certain trail? This can restrict the number or variety of tour products you can offer.

Another area to consider is the economic climate. Travel for most people is a discretionary expense. A downturn in the economy can reduce the number of international or national tourists who will purchase tour products. Although, regional visitation may increase because people vacation closer to home.

Other factors to consider are the strengths and weakness of your business. This review, along with your examination of external opportunities and threats form the basis of a SWOT (Strengths, Weaknesses, Opportunities, Threats) analysis. This was discussed in detail in Chapter 2.

MARKET ANALYSIS - Markets change rapidly. If it has been a year or more since you completed your strategic or last marketing plans, it's time to take a look again at the

Market research helps you learn about prospective customers.

market. New ecotourism products will lure ecotourists to different destinations and activities. People's preferences and travel patterns change. Economic and political climate shifts can have dramatic effects on tourism. Remember the Gulf War? In a matter of months, many adventure travel companies who were heavily marketing offshore destinations found themselves scrambling to locate North American tour operators. With the threat of terrorism, many ecotourist chose not to fly overseas.

To complete your market analysis, there are many sources of market research to access (described in Chapter 2.) Market research will help you learn more about prospective customers. In addition to knowing what type of activities customers are looking for, it is important to know their motivations and trip decisions. Are they being lured to destinations or are they escaping from something, such as a cold North American winter? What time of year do they prefer to travel? What factors influence that choice? In North America, families with children have traditionally favored summer vacations. As some regions move to year-round schooling, people may be travelling at different times of the year. With more two-career households, people are looking for short-term escapes, rather than extended travel. These trends will give way to others. You need to continually monitor them to better position your business.

Market research helps us avoid the tendency to project our likes, dislikes, and habits onto other people, when their backgrounds and preferences may be much different. While you gain valuable information talking to friends and neighbors you need to know what is going on with the travelling public nationally and internationally. Look at information gathered from a large number of people.

When you open for business, you will be deluged with offers to advertise. By doing a thorough market analysis you will be able to determine which advertisers and advertising media are best suitable to reach your clients. If you sell white-water rafting trips on class 5 rivers, you would probably generate more inquiries from an adventure magazine with a young, active readership than a publication aimed at a family market.

When you have completed your market analysis, you will have identified market segments, or types of customers to target. You will know something about their preferences, life-styles, and locations. These market segments are groups of travellers that are:
· Linked by common interests, origins, or demographic information
· Possible to access by marketing to the segment
· Large enough to make marketing efforts worthwhile

Select market segments that are cohesive, yet narrow enough to market to effectively. If you describe a market segment as people over 45 years of age with a general interest in nature, you would need a very broad range of advertising. If you were to further define this segment by geographic region, for example, people living in the Pacific Northwest, or by trip purpose, say organized club tours, your marketing would be more effective. You can target people through regional publications. You could aim advertising efforts at social clubs and conservation groups with large numbers of over 45 year old members.

COMPETITIVE ANALYSIS - Although you feel you have designed a better mousetrap and the world will beat a path to your door, that is not usually the case. Once you have identified your main market segments, you need to look at the next step, the competitive analysis. You have to let people know you have built a better mousetrap (promotion). You also have to see who else is building mousetraps (competitive analysis) and how they may be using your weaknesses to their advantage (Figure 4-2). A review of competitors lets you determine who is also selling ecotourism products and what they are selling. This analysis helps to determine:
  · If the market is too crowded
  · Your competitors' strengths and weaknesses
  · How to distinguish your product
  · Where you can best compete

Who is your competition? Often we think the ecotourism ventures down the road are our competitors. That is not always the case. They are actually potential partners for attracting ecotourists to your community. The competition is the tourism organizations from the other side of the country and other continents. These destinations have well developed marketing programs and in many cases, are trying to attract the same tourists as you.

Financial investors want to know who your competitors are, and how your business differs from theirs.

The other competitors most often overlooked are the attractions not directly related to ecotourism or even tourism in general. Watching television, gardening, casino gambling, and visiting a shopping mall are all activities a potential tourist may choose over a tour with your company. For families, band camp, cheerleader camp, little league, and athletic camps all compete for the same potential customer. This substitution may be more common with regional travellers. It is important that you are aware it exists and plan for it where appropriate.

When preparing a business plan especially for investors, include a section where you identify and describe in some detail (usually a paragraph or two) businesses that are your main competitors. Describe how your business is different and how you are planning to compete in the market. Because tourism related businesses often lack some credibility with banks, you must work hard to illustrate the unique aspects of your business compared to other tourism operations and ways you will take advantage of this.

FIGURE 4-2 "WHEN THE COMPETITION ANALYZES YOU"

Although you will be busy identifying your competitors' weaknesses and ways that you can take advantage of these, give some thought to your own weaknesses. It is difficult to admit your business is less than perfect or destined for anything other than financial success. Take a minute or two, and look at your venture from an outsider's perspective. Are you dependent upon only one or two talented people for your guiding? Do you have only enough cash in the bank to carry you through two or three bad months? Is your targeted market a very small niche, too small to generate sufficient sales? Your competitors will be analyzing your strengths and weaknesses. Make sure you acknowledge your deficiencies, identify ways to try to correct them, or at least, minimize the ways others can use your weaknesses to compete against you.

Look at the whole picture before eliminating potential products. One just might be your ideal product-market match.

PRODUCT-MARKET MATCH - One of the foundations of your marketing plan is the products you sell. After completing the situation analysis, you will know what products you are capable of offering to the traveling public. You may have an abundance of bird life but no accommodations for large groups. This may mean you develop a product for one-day birdwatching trips or multi-day trips with stays at smaller inns or bed and breakfasts.

By looking at all the possible products you can offer, you have a better chance of matching these products with the markets identified in the market analysis. If your research indicates most tourists coming to your area are couples looking for a relaxing weekend retreat, you can focus your marketing on weekend packages. They may include fine dining, bird watching, and sampling homemade jams from local farmers at tea time. Your product-market match will look something like Figure 4-3.

By organizing your most likely market segments and the products you are able to deliver, you can see what you can sell and to whom. This will help you select the best advertising strategy for reaching your target market. This does not mean you will not be thrilled to see a customer from the other side of the globe, but that person is the gravy as opposed to the meat and potatoes of your business. If the number of clients from outside your target market grows noticeably, you have overlooked a segment in your market analysis or are filling a travel need you were not aware of. In either case, revisit your product-market match to see if there is a way of including this new market in your plans.

Marketing objectives provide specific work tasks.

MARKETING OBJECTIVES - As with all business activities, setting objectives provides direction and measures success. Marketing is no different. You need goals and objectives that are measurable, time bound, and realistic. Of these, measurability is the one that causes the greatest number of problems for ecotourism operators. By looking at the goal and objective process in detail, we can see how to better define our objectives to be more successful.

Marketing goals are broad-based, with a high level expectation. An example of a

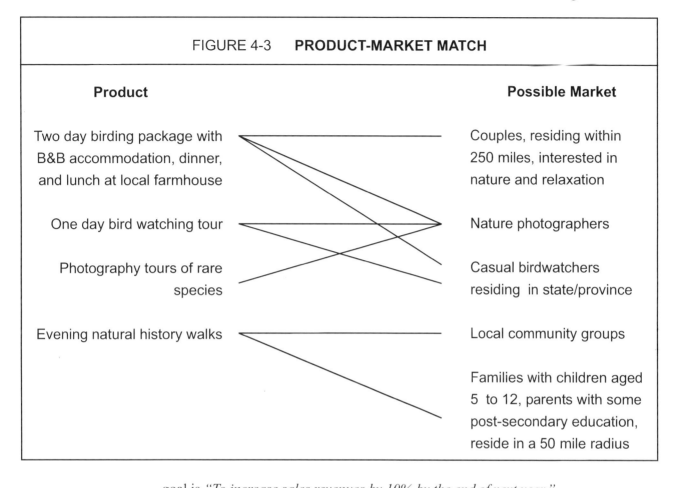

FIGURE 4-3   **PRODUCT-MARKET MATCH**

Product

Two day birding package with B&B accommodation, dinner, and lunch at local farmhouse

One day bird watching tour

Photography tours of rare species

Evening natural history walks

Possible Market

Couples, residing within 250 miles, interested in nature and relaxation

Nature photographers

Casual birdwatchers residing in state/province

Local community groups

Families with children aged 5 to 12, parents with some post-secondary education, reside in a 50 mile radius

goal is *"To increase sales revenues by 10% by the end of next year."*

This does not tell you how to increase revenues but it does set a measurable, time bound and realistic goal. You could use a price increase, sell more products, or change the mix of your products to sell more expensive tours. If the goal had been only to *"Increase Sales,"* it would not tell you how much of an increase or by when. If you sold only one extra dollar worth of ecotours over previous years or months, you would have met your goal.

Marketing objectives follow the same principles as goals but provide specific work tasks or activities needed to reach your overall goals. If my goal is to increase sales revenues by 10% by the end of next year, my objectives may be:

- Increase sales of winter packages by 5 percent for the coming winter.
- Increase sales of weekend hiking trips to social clubs by 20 percent in each of the next three years.
- Increase the number of evening interpretative talks by two for each week from July 1 to September 1.

Use the worksheet in Figure 4-4 to outline your marketing goals and objectives.

Marketing goals are broad-based, with a high level expectation.

FIGURE 4-4 **MARKETING GOAL AND OBJECTIVE WORKSHEET**

Goal:

Example: Increase sales revenues by 10% by the end of next year

_____

_____

_____

Objectives:

Examples:

1. Increase sales of winter packages by 5% for the coming winter.

2. Increase sales of weekend hiking trips to social clubs by 20% in each of the next 3 years.

3. Increase number of evening interpretative talks by 2 for each week from July 1 to September 1.

_____

_____

POSITIONING - Market positioning comes from your competitive analysis. It describes

_____

_____

_____

---

the way you distinguish your business or product from the competition. When considering how to position your products, look for areas where you can develop a unique advantage and compete effectively.

Areas where you can position your business are:

· Price

· Quality

· Service

· Location and access

· Ability to customize

Of these, price is probably the least desirable area to compete. If you decide to

Price is probably the least desirable area to compete.

position yourself by offering the lowest price, chances are there will be someone else who can offer a lower price than you. They may be using a competitive product to attract customers for other reasons and have the resources to sell it at a lose. You may find that your customers are not loyal and will use another ecotour firm just based on a lower price. A better approach is to position yourself through quality service and promote your company as offering the best value versus the best price.

Some ecotourism businesses may be able to position their business as leaders in product or service quality. This approach requires tremendous effort to ensure all areas of your operation meet established standards. There will likely be additional start-up and operating costs. These costs may be recovered against higher prices if you truly offer superior quality. Abercrombie and Kent is a tour company that chose quality and service strategies as the basis for their positioning in the marketplace. A customer who selects one of their tours, a wildlife-viewing safari to east Africa, will stay at resorts of exceptional quality, travel in comfort, and be led by some of the most knowledgeable guides in the country.

Service is the easiest way to position your product.

Service for many ecotourism businesses, is the easiest way to position their product. With guides and support staff who are consistently courteous, friendly, and attentive to the ecotourist needs, you will distinguish yourself as a company that delivers great customer service. Do not forget interpretation is a critical component of a ecotour. This is also an obvious way to better position your product.

The next area of positioning strategies is your location or access. If you are located in or have access to a unique location, use this fact as a way to set you apart from other destinations or tours. Ecotourists seek uniqueness and remoteness locations. Although not a consumptive users of wildlife, in some ways ecotourist like to have "trophy experiences". Being the first to visit a destination or undertaking a unique activity like sea kayaking in the high Arctic, provides a type of status and satisfy their need for variety.

The ability to customize a trip is another way to position your business. Ecotourists like variety, unique experiences and flexibility. If your client can choose from several activities or locations to customize their own package, it will be more attractive to them. Ecotourism companies have found customized packages popular with their clients and a way to distinguished their business from others.

MARKETING STRATEGIES - Once you have defined your goals and objectives, you will know what marketing success will look like. To achieve that success, you need to develop specific actions or strategies to increase awareness and attractiveness of your product so travellers are motivated to buy (see Figure 4-5). These strategies spell out what will be done by whom to reach your desired goals. Start with the four Ps of marketing - product, price, placement, and promotion.

All four are equally important in the marketing mix.

FIGURE 4-5 **SELL TO A FEELING**

When advertising, take the time to develop an advertisement or "copy" that sells. The most important thing you can do is to sell to a feeling. People want to hear about the personal benefits of a tour, not necessarily the specific features. The decision to take a particular trip is often based upon emotion. If you can attract the customer's eye (or ear) with an emotional appeal while providing reasons why they would benefit from your trip, you have a better chance of making a sale.

People buy trips for a variety of reasons: to escape from something, to satisfy curiosity, to spend time with family, to meet new friends. The list is a long one. Focus on the personal reasons why people might take a trip and explain how your ecotourism experience will satisfy their needs.

When describing the benefits your customers will enjoy, include information to overcome objections such as:

- Lack of time or money
- A belief they do not "need" your trip
- A fear it may not be the right experience for them
- Skepticism about your claims

Think about including a guarantee in your advertisement. You can remove some of the apprehension by offering a refund or a chance to travel again. One whale-watching company offers a guarantee that deals with the fear people have of not seeing a whale. If no whales are spotted on a particular sailing, customers can take another trip at no additional cost.

For more information on writing copy, talk to people who have lots of experience in the field. A good source is Joe Vitale, the author of *The 21 Most Powerful Copywriting Rules of All Time* who can be accessed on the internet at http://www.mrfire.com.

- Product
- Price
- Placement
- Promotion

The following sections discuss the development of these strategies in more detail.

Your choice of product possibilities are endless.

Product may involve a physical good (baskets crafted by an indigenous tribe) and/or a service (offering nature viewing tours in a unique setting). The possibilities are endless and have been discussed in detail throughout this book.

Price is what you charge for a product. A well thought out pricing strategy can be used to distinguish your product from competitors. When setting a price, it is important to consider the various types of competition in your target market. If your competitors all seem to be trying to under bid one and another, then perhaps the best strategy is to offer a product of higher quality and with better service. You will then be able to target your product to an upscale market, complete with an higher price tag.

When setting pricing policies, it is also important to consider customer reaction to possible prices. If customers feel your product does not justify the higher price, then the product or price needs to be adjusted accordingly or all of your efforts will be wasted.

Placement is concerned with getting the right product to the target market. What method(s) will you use to distribute your product? The methods you choose must be both cost effective and efficient for you to survive.

Many ecotourism businesses sell their products or services directly to the traveller. The advantages of direct selling include saving money on commissions and being a fairly simple process to start. Through the marketing activities discussed in the following sections, you can promote your product directly to the ecotourist in the hope they will book a trip.

However, relying strictly on direct selling to reach all your market segments is costly in both money and time. Many ecotour operators who have found direct sales too difficult to manage have turned to specialized businesses who sell tourism products. These travel intermediaries include tour wholesalers or operators, travel agents, and destination marketing organizations. Intermediaries can be an effective way to supplement your own direct marketing efforts. Or, you may choose to rely solely on them to sell your product.

Using travel trade intermediaries also has its disadvantages. They expect a fee or commission for selling your product. Often there is a need for long lead times to promote your tours or facility. Tour wholesalers may already have sufficient suppliers in your region and are not interested in adding another ecotourism product. But if you do find one, it may take 18 to 24 months to develop and sell the product. Many ecotour operators dislike selling and assume a travel agent can do much of the selling. However, if the agent is not familiar with the ecotourism market or has easier products to sell, little or no products may be sold. For more information on travel intermediaries, see Chapters 5 and 6.

Promotion When you have set your marketing objectives and selected strategies to sell your product, it is time to turn to marketing activities. Promotion is concerned with telling the target market about your product. It includes personal selling, mass distribution, and sales promotion. These are the most visible parts of the marketing process and new

There are many things that must be considered when setting price.

Methods you use to distribute your product must be cost effective and efficient.

Promotion is telling the target market about your product.

business owners may skip directly to this step without defining objectives and analyzing the market. This is not a cost-effective way of selling your product and could be fatal for your business. There are many promotional and advertising activities that can be used.

- Direct sales
- Brochures
- Video
- Internet
- Signage

- Print media (directories, newspapers, magazines)
- Trade shows
- Conferences
- Television/Radio
- Publicity

What theme or image do you want to project?

Before you undertake any of these activities, give some thought to the theme or image you want to promote. This theme will be the main image or message you leave with potential customers. Identifying a theme early on will keep your marketing activities focused and help an ecotourist form a clear picture of your company.

Your theme needs to focus on the areas where you have decided to position your business. If you offer friendly service, you may emphasize fun and new activities your trips provide. If you take people to undiscovered and out-of-the-way places, use that as your theme. A company that prides itself on low impact travel practices would emphasize its compatibility with nature.

Your theme forms the basis for slogans in promotions. It helps to organize your messages and pictures on printed material. It influences the type of advertising activities you use. To get feedback on the clarity of your message, provide copies of your promotional material to others. Ask them what images come to mind when they look at your materials. Ask customers what comes to mind when they think of your company. You may be surprised. If you view yourself as a company with access to remote hiking sites, you may be amazed to find out people choose your trips for a chance to meet other people with similar interests. When potential customers consider your company for reasons other than what you expect, it could mean you are not getting your message across, or you are offering more important benefits to travellers than you realized. Either way, you need to learn more about your customers and the travel experience they are looking for.

MARKETING ACTIVITIES - The following sections describe ways to get your marketing messages to potential customers.

Direct Sales means selling directly to the customer via telephone, fax, mail, or in person. This could include mailing your brochure to prospective customers. It could take the form of a facsimile to past customers, letting them know about upcoming tours. Calling or visiting customers is part of direct sales. All are relevant for ecotourism businesses.

When entering the direct sales arena, it is important to stay focused. You must target your most important market segments. When doing a direct mailing, use a qualified mailing list which is based on some characteristic meaningful to your target market, thus containing a large number of potential customers. A mailing list from a conservation group is likely a good start because everyone on the list has an interest in conservation. Market research has shown many ecotourists belong to nature associations or conservation groups. However, a list taken from the Omaha, Nebraska phone book would have little benefit unless you have determined that proximity to Omaha is a key characteristic to your market segment.

When entering the direct sales arena, it is important to stay focused.

Once a potential list is identified, you will want to test it by doing a mailing to a portion of the list, say 10 percent. Monitor the response from this mailing. If you achieve a response rate greater than seven per cent, then increase the mailing, perhaps to everyone on the list. Qualified mailing lists can generate business but you will pay for using them. Remember to include this cost in your marketing budget. Depending upon the size of the list and the type of organization, the cost starts at approximately $100 and goes higher. Members of tourism or recreation organizations may be able to obtain their mailing lists for a reduced fee.

Direct sales by telephone and in person are more relevant for ecotourism businesses when selling to groups, wholesalers, and packagers. Mailing to these groups without follow up is not effective, so the use of phone calls or personal visits is needed. Because of the labor and travel costs, direct sales calls and visits are relatively expensive. However, the opportunity exists to sell a large number of tours to one organization. It is important to research the prospective client thoroughly, ensuring that they fit your market segment profile.

Remember, the customer base built through direct sales will provide you with personal referrals. Research studies show that ecotourists rely on word-of-mouth as the best way to learn about products. Keep your company and its offerings in front of your past customers so they remember to recommend you.

Brochures (sometimes called lure brochures) are sales tools used to inform visitors about your ecotourism product and region. Useful and relatively inexpensive, they make good handouts, can be used to respond to inquiries, and to support promotional displays and presentations.

A savvy ecotourist will be looking for information, not fluff.

When developing a brochure, remember your themes and the need to sell to an emotion. There are many good references on the internet and at the library. Also consult with people who have experience with writing copy and desktop design, such as a local printer, for tips on designing printed material.

The steps for developing brochures are:

1. Identify your objectives - Who will receive it? How will they get it? What message will you present? What response are you looking for?

2. Determine what combination of text, illustrations, and/or photographs is best to convey your product information
3. Write the copy for the brochure
4. Create a mock-up
5. Get feedback on mock-up and adjust as needed
6. Obtain camera ready artwork
7. Print

Start by picking up brochures of other businesses and analyze them. Look for things that work and do not work. Incorporate the elements into your brochure which help sell your product. Do not cover every square centimeter with text and graphics. Leave plenty of white space so it is easy to read and pleasing to the eye, not jumbled and confusing. Include photographs and illustrations to illustrate key points.

Leave plenty of white space so copy is easy to read and pleasing to the eye.

A savvy ecotourist will be looking for information, not fluff, and wants to be convinced you offer a quality nature or cultural experience. Include photographs and descriptions of the area visited and key elements of the trip. Information on the interpretation component or qualifications of the guides is important to most ecotourists. You should mention any partnerships or alliances with conservation groups. By the time someone is looking at your brochure, they have already shown an interest in your region and business. To complete the sale, you need to convince them you have the key elements they are looking for in an ecotourism experience.

The appearance of the brochure is also important. People may be expecting to see a recycled paper consistent with an your business's commitment to the environment. Glossy paper can be a problem with some ecotourists. With the quality of recycled paper rapidly improving, you can now produce color brochures on recycled paper that rival that of bleached, virgin papers.

Once your brochures are produced, you will want to get them into the hands of potential customers. You can distribute brochures at:

· Consumer and trade shows
· Visitor bureaus and tourist information centers
· Hotels and motels
· Shopping malls

A disturbing trend in the distribution of tourism brochures is paying for distribution services. In the past, ecotourism operators could distribute through tourist information centers. With the move towards financial self-sufficiency, tourist information centers operated by government or quasi-government agencies sometimes charge a fee to distribute brochures. Inquire with the tourist information centers you wish to use as to their policy. You may want to find alternative distribution venues or budget additional funds.

Video can be used to supplement printed material, however, its use should be approached with caution. It can be another great tool at events such as trade shows where their visual appeal can draw potential customers to your display. For smaller organizations, the cost of producing a video is too expensive to be viable. While it may be possible to use the video as internet advertising, most users will not have the equipment nor the time to do so.

The cost of pro-ducing a video is often too expensive to be viable.

If you decide to do a video, use the same guidelines we discussed for developing printed material. Again the key to success is to determine the objectives of the video and how they relate to the target market.

Planning and forethought are key to get an acceptable return on your investment of time and money. Determine what scenes will best convey your message. You may want footage of visitors enjoying your tours. Show employees undertaking activities that make your business environmentally friendly. Or, highlight a design element of your lodge that lessens its environmental footprint and impacts.

Internet is the most important tourism marketing method. Many tourist businesses are using it as a low-cost way to advertise their services globally because internet users fit the ecotourists profile. The internet has the advantage of allowing small business web sites to look just as professional as large business' site. This advantage is offset by the fact that people must first find your web site and will spend time at it only if there is something interesting. Unlike a bad radio ad sandwiched between good programming and heard by a "captive audience," this is not the case with the internet. If your site is difficult to access, slow to upload, lacks information, or badly organized, your potential customer is gone in a matter of seconds and may never return. With over 80 million pages and growing, your site must meet your target markets' needs to be of any value to them and you.

The internet is only one part of your marketing mix.

Internet is also an environmentally-friendly way to disseminate information. People can learn about your product without the paper required for brochures or fuel used to transport mail.

If you decide to use the internet as a promotional tool, remember your overall marketing objective is to derive maximum use from exciting technology. The internet is only one part of the marketing mix and should support other promotional activities. When developing a site, consider the following:

1. <u>Purpose</u>. Determine how internet technology will support your marketing objectives. If you can achieve your objectives through other media, or if your market is primarily local, you may find an internet presence most effective for

increasing product awareness rather than for generating bookings. Organizations seeking to compete in foreign markets may use the internet as their main access to these markets.

Web pages that load slowly lose viewers quickly.

2. <u>Content</u>. Use pictures, text, even sound to get your message across. You are selling an experience so the use of pictures and sound can be very effective. The use of podcasting is growng rapidly and is easy to use, even for small business. Multimedia files added to your website allow for things like customer testimonials in a more vivid format than text or descriptions of special trip experience. Be sure the use of pictures and graphics are used appropriately. Too many images in the wrong format (tif vs jpg) will result in an extended upload time. A home page that takes forever (one minute or more) to load will result in lost viewers. People get impatient quickly, especially if there is little value to them. Internet users are looking for information, not advertising. Make sure your site has valuable information for the target market that changes over time. You need to give people a reason to return to your site throughout the year.

3. <u>Design</u>. Your home page, like print media, needs to be well organized and stay true to your marketing objectives. Use formatting, a variety of fonts, and graphics to make your site visually appealing. Link to other home pages to add depth to your site and provides more useful information. Such links may include destinations, equipment manufactures or birding sites. Swapping links also helps direct people to your site. Consider other ways to make your page unique, after all there are millions of web sites to choose from. What will make people visit your site? One ecotourism operator incorporates updates on wildlife research so people will visit frequently for current information. This also provides exposure for wildlife researchers, who are often looking for financial support for projects, a good example of a partnership between business and conservation groups.

Technology will affect your ability to design your internet presence and the ease with which people can retrieve information.

4. <u>Technology</u>. An existing or prospective client's ability to find you on the web is critical. Over the last decade the web has gone from a curiosity to a "must use" technology. Many people use the web as their sole means of finding recreation and vacation opportunities. Without a web site you do not exist for many people worldwide.

Having a site does not have to mean spending thousands of dollars for development and design. With a little help from your area technical school you can design, author and host a simple site for as little as USD$9.95 a month. Some schools offer workshops or facilities for you to develop your own home page. Be aware of the fast paced changes, do not try every new feature. Make sure your page is compatible with the abilities and wants of your target markets. You can also contract with a local internet service provider for your web page development. Just make sure you have (in writing) the services to be provided and the cost.

Modem speeds can greatly affect the way your page is viewed by a potential customer. Pages with large graphics files, plug-ins, sound, etc., download slowly. Many internet users will not wait for more then 30 seconds before they move on and never return, resulting in a lost opportunity. As we move into the next millennium, the number of pages available has gone from millions to billions. Needless to say your site may be nearly impossible for users to find. Marketing your site is very important. Strategies include getting listed in many different search engines, swapping links, pay-per-click, being liked to associations, chamber of commerce, and local and regional tourism pages. All your marketing efforts should have your email and web address prominently displayed.

There are more aspects to a successful website then we can cover here. For more information, talk to your area trade associations, local internet provider, read many of the great online websites or attend a course at your local technical college.

5. <u>Access.</u> Once you have developed a web page you must consider how people will find you on the internet. With more and more pages on the web, it is becoming difficult to establish a presence. Some experts in fact, have estimated it can cost millions of dollars to develop an internet identity!

While search engines are touted as a critical part of being located online, their use is becoming more cumbersome as hundreds of thousands of web sites are added each year. A single search can generate hundreds or thousands of matches for a search term, discouraging for the traveler looking for your product. To make it easier to find your online advertising, you may try pay-per-click or linking with established web sites or rely on word of mouth referrals, email style. Many web sites are adding "postcards" that allow people to tell their friends about great web addresses they have found. And of course, don't forget to add your web site address to all of your print material. As one Generation Xer stated, "without a website address on travel brochure I wouldn't know where to look for more information."

Another option you may want to consider is listing your ecotourism product with a larger web site that helps people plan their next vacation. If people know about you, they will likely find your web site. But to attract a broader range of people who may not have heard of you or who haven't decided if they will travel to Minnesota or Mongolia, undertake cave exploration or kayaking, a listing on a larger service may be appropriate. These listings are not always cheap, some will charge an annual fee, some charge per "click" to your site, others charge a commission based on business created, so shop around before you pick the best internet partners for you. Try to think of your Internet presence as a stock portfolio, you will need diversity to make it work. With good planning, you will find like many operators, that the Internet is replacing traditional forms of marketing.

Signage - Signs can attract tourists to your ecotourism property and provide interpretation once they arrive. For ecotourism businesses offering tours, signs may not be as important as for a lodge or an attraction. In most cases you need signs on highways, access roads, and entrances. Signs should tell people what services you offer and direct them to your business. At your site, you may need interpretative signs to create interest in unique natural or cultural history items.

Signs are an extension of what you are.

When developing signs make sure they fit within the overall framework of your marketing plan. Signs are an extension of what you are. A large plastic sign with flashing lights may not be what you want at an elegant log structure in a wooded setting. Also using wood obtained from rainforests, redwoods, or similar trees may be unacceptable to your customers. If your visitors arrive by air and are shuttled to your remote lodge by employees, you do not need extensive or elaborate signs.

Once you have designed them, obtain approval for the signs at the appropriate levels of government. This may require some compromise on your part, depending on local ordinances. Once approved, construct, install, and maintain it. A broken, dirty, or poorly maintained sign does not give anyone a favorable impression of your facility.

Print Media - The use of print media is one of the most important marketing activities your ecotourism business will undertake. Although price varies with the format, print media is cost effective, and it will generate sales for tourism businesses if the message, type, and timing are well planned. It will often be your main method of communicating with potential customers, as you can reach many people with relatively little effort. For example, a print ad in the right directory can put your ecotourism business in front of thousands of travelers who you could never contact otherwise.

Always get the free publicity first!

Print media encompasses directory listings, brochures, newspaper, and magazine advertisements. You will likely use other forms of marketing, but there is a strong possibility that you will need to rely on some print media to let people know about you. Although many ecotourists make their decisions by word-of-mouth, you need to bring in enough customers at start-up and to supplement your word of mouth referrals.

Each print medium has advantages and disadvantages. The best way to select the appropriate media is to review your market research and target market trends. Remember, do not undertake paid advertising until you have completed your public-relations program. Always get the free publicity first!

1. <u>Directories</u>. As soon as you have thrown open the doors of your business, you will be approached by companies who want you to advertise in their directory. A directory is a listing of businesses that have something in common. Often tourism directories are organized by geographic region or activity. You may encounter a directory that lists accommodations, attractions, and activities for a particular state or a region within a state. If you run a bed and breakfast with great bird watching, there are directories that list nothing but bed and breakfasts. Even the yellow pages is a directory for businesses with telephones.

   Whether or not you advertise in directories should be based upon the following factors:

   · Does my potential customer use this directory?
   · How is this directory distributed?
   · How many copies are made?
   · How often is it updated ?
   · What is the cost for a listing?

   Some state or provincial tourism departments do a very good job of producing and distributing directories outlining accommodations, attractions, and activities. These often have a broad distribution, so this may be a good way to get your ecotourism product advertised. These publications may require you to be in business a year or two before you can be listed. The publisher is looking for some indication that the companies listed are established and will be in business when customers arrive.

2. <u>Newspapers</u>. Hear yea! Hear yea! Get your daily paper! Lots of people read newspapers, and advertising in them may be a good way to reach segments of your market. Before buying newspaper advertising, consider again your objectives and market segments. Newspapers will be most effective in attracting people from a regional market or urban center, if a large part of your business originates there.

   An effective way to use newspaper advertisements is by consortium opportunities. If a travel writer is doing a story on your region or business, taking out an advertisement in that one issue may be just what you need to sell trips. As well, several nature-based tourism operators may band together to do a special advertising feature on their travel products or services. These types of marketing partnerships can be quite effective because you create a larger, more noticeable presence in the newspaper while sharing the cost. You do not need to plan as far in advance as you would with directory and magazine advertising. This is an advantage when a special opportunity arises and you need to reach your customers quickly. If you are offering

Newspapers are most effective to reach people from a regional or urban center.

a series of summer hikes and need more bookings, you can quickly advertise in the spring when people are making vacation plans.

The down side of newspaper advertising is cost. It is reasonable to assume that since ecotourists are well educated and well read they read newspapers. However, it may take several ads before people actually make a reservation. Advertising rates in major newspapers can be out of reach for many small businesses. One way to manage this is to look at smaller newspapers with lower rates or partner with others to share the cost.

3. Magazines. Magazine advertising can be an important part of your marketing activities. Research has shown ecotourists read a variety of natural history publications, so advertising there will get your message into their homes. Some of these magazines are *Explore, National Geographic Traveler, Outpost, Outside, and Ecotravel.*

Again, the down side is the cost. An advertisement in a national or international publication can cost hundreds or thousands of dollars for one issue. To get results, you may need to run the ad more than once. One way to reduce costs is to purchase a listing instead of a display ad. This is less expensive while still getting your company in front of qualified customers. Also consider regional magazines. They normally have lower advertising rates and can provide better coverage with your target market, especially if most of your customers come from a local area.

Research has shown ecotourists can be reached via a variety of natural history magazines.

An approach that has worked for some ecotourism businesses is to target women's and life-style magazines. Many women's magazines include sections on things to do with the family. If you have a unique activity for a busy woman to spend time with her family, the magazine may publish it at no cost. Getting this coverage can be a labor intensive experience with little control over the coverage you receive.

Another approach is to work with travel writers to have your business featured or mentioned in an article. This form of promotion is far more effective than paid advertising. Attracting a travel writer usually has some associated cost. There may be an expectation all or part of the trip cost will be waived for their participation on your trips. You should research the credentials of the writer and publication to ensure an article will benefit your organization.

Trade Shows - Displaying at trade shows can be another effective marketing activity. Select trade shows based on your target market and distribution methods and the show's ability to provide the best links to your target audiences. If you use intermediaries, your trade show activities and display should focus on industry contacts and product benefits.

If selling directly to the consumer, use consumer trade shows that focus on leisure and travel for quick access to large numbers of interested people. Again, the focus needs to address their needs and wants, relaxation, unique experience, or adventure. Some of the large trade shows that may be of interest are the ITB Berlin, the Adventures in Travel Expo, the World Travel Mart (London), and the Adventure Travel World Summit.

Many states and provinces also hold trade shows to promote regional tourism. Contact your local tourism or economic-development organizations for a list of upcoming trade shows and contact information. Many tourism bureaus or marketing boards attend trade shows and encourage local businesses to attend as part of a larger group. This is a good way to generate attention and credibility for your product, especially at the large trade shows where a small operator can get lost in the shuffle while reducing trade show cost.

Attending trade shows can be an expensive undertaking. Travel and display space cost are only the beginning. You may be required to pay workers to set up and take down your exhibits. Then there may be a fee for table coverings, tables, chairs, electricity, backdrop, just to name just a few. If you are going to another country, a customs broker may be needed to assist in shipping promotional material across borders. Include all of this in your marketing budget and think long term. You will need to attend a particular show for several years to develop name recognition and see the benefits of increased bookings.

Once committed to attending a trade show, give thought to your display. As the goal of attending a trade show is to sell your product or to network with other industry people, you want a display to attract attendees and convey the selling points of your ecotour. Increase the odds of people stopping by having a special point of interest as part of the display. Some displayers have found that having a nut mixture is the best way to get people to linger at their booth! Be creative. Remember, this is an extension of your business image, make it a good one.

One part of the trade show routine most forgotten are the workers manning the booth. They are your ambassadors and welcome committee. First impressions are everything. Bring your best. Make sure you have enough staff to give people breaks to rest, eat, and for other necessities including seeing the show. They need to maintain a fresh, friendly, and professional appearance in order to make that sale.

As you meet people provide them with your brochures, business cards, or other promotional material. Take the time to briefly explain your unique features and answer questions. Explain the great experience they will have. This will keep your business in their minds when they make vacation plans. If they show an interest ask them to fill out a sign-up sheet so you can provide additional information by mail or phone. Then do the needed follow-up after the show. Asking for business cards or having a prize

Displaying at trade shows can be another effective marketing activity.

Your trade show workers are your ambassadors and welcome committee. Bring your best.

drawing will help build up your contact list. If possible, code the information you handed out, so you can monitor the sales that ultimately arise. Talk to people who have already attended these trade shows to find out what works and what doesn't. Attending trade shows costs time and money. Attend only those trade shows that reach your target market and will generate significant bookings.

Conferences - There are many conferences that deal with tourism in general, as well as a number that pertain directly to ecotourism, such as the North American Conference on Ecotourism, the Educational Travel Conference, and the Watchable Wildlife Conference.

Conferences are unlikely to generate new business, unless there is a trade show attached. Their main purpose is to keep you informed on industry developments, generate ideas for new products and marketing strategies, and help make new contacts. Partnerships are an effective way of stretching your marketing dollars. Conferences are the place to meet people with similar businesses or from the same geographic regions, and can be a good place to form worthwhile partnerships.

Offer to speak at conferences you will attend. You will gain great visibility for your business (all of it free promotion) and in many cases, you will receive a break on conference fees.

Conferences keep you informed, generate ideas, and provide networking opportunities.

Television/Radio - Television and radio may not be appropriate for many ecotourism businesses. The short message time, 30 to 60 seconds, does not lend itself easily to influencing a major vacation decision. However, they can be used to promote special events, rates, or season opening in the local area. This media is more appropriate for a ecotourism attraction.

You may get free television coverage by approaching community, education or science and nature channels. These channels are always looking for new programming ideas; your ecotourism product or service may appeal to them as a way to highlight nature discovery in the community.

While television may be too expensive for you, radio can be a cost-effective alternative. Radio is most beneficial for advertising special events or packages to local markets.

Television and radio are useful in promoting special events.

With radio and television advertising, you have little control over when your advertisement is played. Often you are guaranteed air play within a specified block of time which may be several hours long. You may feel your advertisement has been played when no potential customers are listening. If you are willing to pay added fees, you can get specific time-slots, such as the evening news. The cost for this service is much higher and must be weighed against other advertising options.

Publicity - One of the best ways to make your marketing dollars go farther is free (or almost free advertising) publicity. While you will incur some labor, postage, and stationary costs, if you have put careful thought into a publicity campaign, you can gain public attention and support for next to nothing. Obtaining free coverage through radio, television, magazines, other businesses' flyers and newsletters, and tourist bureaus all can enhance the image of your business.

To obtain maximum publicity, you will need a plan. Although there is no significant financial cost to most publicity, you still need to determine who your target markets are, media to approach, what are you doing that is newsworthy, and how can you help the media provide coverage. The most critical element is having a "news angle". Without that your story is unlikely to be considered by any media. If you are a for-profit business, present your activities in a way that is news, not a promotion. This can include information of new staff, awards, implementing new policies, special activities, or human interest stories about special clients. If you are doing a trip for the disadvantaged, disabled, local school, etc, invite the media to attend. Editors are in the business of providing news coverage, not free advertising.

To obtain maximum publicity, you will need a plan.

When writing a news release, include information on the unique features of your organization. For example, you are the first tourism business to develop a comprehensive environmental education policy in your region. Include a human interest element. This is an important criteria used by editors when trying to determine which stories to cover. Your human interest element may be the school children who receive conservation talks and demonstration from your company's guides.

Do not forget to include the 5 Ws (who, what, where, when, why) in your press release. However, it is best to cover only one main thought in the release. Adding too many items causes confusion and minimizes your chance for coverage. You may also want to convey a sense of immediacy to the event, so it has a news quality that media will miss if they do not cover the story. Include background information on your organization in the latter parts of the press release or as a separate item.

If the thought of writing a press release leaves you a bit nervous, there are companies whose specialty is getting businesses free publicity. Some of these people come from the news industry and have a good idea of what an editor is looking for. For a flat fee, they will write your press releases and send them to appropriate people at newspapers, magazines, radio stations, and television stations. They will also assist in obtaining public-service announcements.

Remember that publicity is advertising over which you have little control. You do not get to approve the story before it goes to the public. If they have incorrect information or are following an angle that you had not counted on, there is little you can do. Preparing a press kit that provides background information on your ecotourism product can help avoid errors arising from ignorance, but the slant that a news organization puts on your story can be a surprise, and in some cases, cast a negative light. In those situations, consider it a learning experience and vow to work more closely with the media so they have a clearer understanding of what you represent.

Ecotourism businesses are in a good position to generate publicity because of these human interest element and the benefits ecotourism provides. One ecotourism company in Alberta, Canada, took a local news anchorman on a snowshoeing trip. The trip and the antics of the anchorman received significant coverage on the weekend news. It gave the television station a chance to show something "new and interesting" in a way that was entertaining to viewers and the ecotourism operator got exposure over a very large audience.

If you are at all literary, consider writing a newspaper column as a way to get your name in front of people. If you write a column on local wildlife or recreational activities, you will establish yourself as an expert in the field. This will work best if you contribute on a regular basis and write about topics that are of interest to local readers. Another approach is to establish relationships with reporters and editors as an expert source for background information and for quotes. Become the area expert to call with the question. Being able to comment on tourism trends and activities, or culture and natural history, may put your name in front of local audiences several times a year.

Remember, publicity is advertising over which you have little control.

MARKETING BUDGETS

After you develop your marketing plan, you need to account for the cost of these activities in either your start up or operating budget for the upcoming year. Look at the various market segments identified and the activities selected for each. Your activities for the current year, and future years if appropriate, should have costs estimated in some detail.

A worksheet you can use for your marketing budget is shown in Table 4-1. As you gather information, you may be dismayed at the cost of promoting your business and find that you will not have the funds to market your business as you would like. There are a couple of approaches you can take in this situation. Consider marketing partnerships where you join with other businesses to promote your destination. This is discussed in chapter 6. Another approach is to carefully evaluate past marketing efforts and put your money into those activities that generated the highest yield. If you have no history or have not monitored your marketing programs, you can start by identifying what information you need now and determine how you will collect it in the future.

FORECASTING SALES

In your marketing plan, you set goals and objectives for each market segment you targeted. Using this information, you will forecast the sales levels you expect for the next year and perhaps the next three to five years. This sales forecast is a starting point for other financial forecasts and analysis. Gathering information on the cost of your business is relatively straightforward, predicting your sales revenues is much more difficult. To make the process easier and increase the accuracy of your forecasts use the following techniques.

REVIEW HISTORICAL SALES INFORMATION. While the past is not a predictor of the future, looking at the level of sales both in terms of dollars and number of trips sold, can be very helpful in identifying trends. You may notice that trips featuring aboriginal heritage have been popular and feel confident the popularity will increase. This would lead you to forecast a larger number of trips than in past years.

EXTRAPOLATE SALES FORECASTS FROM PRIMARY RESEARCH RESULTS. If you were able to conduct primary market research in the past year or two, you can use that research to estimate sales. Market research on nature or culture-based tourism done at a state or regional level can also be used to forecast sales levels. As market research ages, it is less useful in pinpointing exact numbers but may still offer good information on trends.

GATHER INFORMATION FROM COMPETITORS AND SUPPLIERS. Competitors may be willing to provide you information in exchange for information on your operation. If a competitor is expecting a large increase in the number of FITs (fully independent travellers) for natural history hikes, consider increasing your sales forecasts from last year's level for comparable tours. Suppliers also have helpful information on who is doing what in the industry, and some of it may affect your business. If you talk to the company that rents kayaks, they can give you some idea as to how busy they expect their year to be, the anticipated length of rental they anticipate, and the type of customers, whether independent travellers or tour packagers.

TALK TO TOURISM AGENCIES, such as destination marketing organizations (DMOs), such as the regional chamber of commerce, division/department of tourism, visitors bureaus and planning commissions, monitor trends to determine the regions and countries that are growth markets, the product types tourists are seeking, and the best way to market destinations to high-yield groups. Not all the markets targeted by DMOs will be of interest to you, but, their activities have some relevance to your sales. If they are target-

TABLE 4-1 MARKETING BUDGET			
CATEGORY	YEAR 1	YEAR 2	YEAR 3
DIRECT SALES	$	$	$
direct mail			
direct sales - fax			
direct sales - telephone			
direct sales - in person			
BROCHURES			
brochure development			
brochure printing			
INTERNET			
internet development			
internet maintenance			
VIDEO			
SIGNAGE			
PRINT MEDIA			
directories			
newspaper ads			
magazine			
TRADE SHOWS			
registration			
travel costs			
CONFERENCES			
conference fees			
travel costs			
TELEVISION/RADIO			
television			
radio			
PUBLICITY			
press kits & releases			
complimentary items			
FAMILIARISATION TOURS			
travel writers			
travel agents			
wholesalers			
packagers			
COUPONS (revenue foregone)			
MARKET RESEARCH			
MONITORING			
TOTAL MARKETING COSTS			

ing large tour groups in the Japanese market, it could mean you will not benefit, as the travel patterns of these groups (large numbers, very structured itineraries, little time in one place) are not consistent with most ecotourism products. A DMO marketing to the German market may bring people into the area that are very interested in a nature-based tourism product, thus increasing your sales opportunities.

Talk to customers. By asking your customer base what their travel plans are and monitoring requests for brochures and trip itineraries, you will have some idea as to how many past customers will be traveling with you in the upcoming year.

After reviewing these sources, you will still be guessing at sales levels to a certain extent. By gathering information from as many sources as possible and cross-checking your findings, you increase the probability that your sales targets are reasonable. Use the format in Table 4-2 to aid your financial forecasting and analyze numbers for reasonability. Modify it to match the uniqueness of your product. Add additional lines for each type of tour or to distinguish between different prices, such as low-season and peak-season. The forecast format refers to number of tours or number of tour days. If your business offers accommodations or is an attraction, use it to forecast number of bed nights or number of visitors.

MONITORING AND EVALUATING MARKETING ACTIVITIES

After selecting marketing tools and forecasting sales, consider how to evaluate your marketing effectiveness. You may develop your marketing plan and through its implementation, have a very successful year. You will still want to know which parts of your marketing plan were most effective. Did your appearance at the ITB trade show generate sales? Did you advertise in a directory that was not distributed to your market segment? These things happen. Keep track of what business is generated by each marketing activity and the cost of each activity.

A main component of the monitoring effort is tracking the number of inquiries and bookings resulting from each marketing activity. In its simplest form, ask each person that calls for information or makes a reservation how they heard of you. If you collect data in sufficient detail, for example, the name and issue of the magazine where they saw your advertisement, you will be well on the way to evaluating your marketing plan.

Staff may not always query callers in detail and customers do not always remember how they heard of you. Coding your marketing efforts can help. If you have an 800 number, you can have people ask for "operators" that correspond to specific advertisements. An advertisement in the *New York Times* may have an Operator 22 next to the telephone number. When a person calls asking for Operator 22, you know they saw your advertisement in the *New York Times*. You can be even more specific by coding the operator to advertisements placed on certain days.

Special prices or offers also can help track where people have heard of your business. If you have a nature walk that costs $40 for three hours, and offer a "special" rate of $39.95. If the advertisement is mentioned, it would tell you the publication or directory that person had read. This can also be used to determine the effectiveness of a radio or television ad related to a specific time, program, or date.

Another component of tracking your marketing effectiveness is to ensure your costs are recorded in a manner that makes analysis possible. If you record all your marketing costs to one account called "marketing" you will have a difficult task evaluating your marketing programs. At the very least, separate marketing expenditures into the same categories as your budget. If you have a large outlay with a specific product or advertisement, set up a separate account for it. Discuss these needs with your accountant so they can set up a reporting system that will enable you to evaluate your marketing plan quickly and easily.

When evaluating marketing program effectiveness look at some of the financial performance indicators you use to evaluate your business as a whole. Some of the most useful are cost per inquiry, cost per visitor, and return on investment. The formulas, shown in Figure 4-5, are simple to apply; the difficulty is in gathering the information. If you do not have detailed information, estimate where possible. For example, if you spent $4,000 to advertise in *Escape* magazine and you received 100 inquiries that led to 10 bookings, cost per inquiry is $40 ($4,000/100) and cost per visitor is $400 ($4,000/ 10).

TABLE 4 - 2 SALES FORCAST

SALES FORECAST FOR THE YEAR OF 2008

	Jan.	Feb.	March	April	May	June	July	Aug.	Sept.	Oct.	Dec.	Total
Sales Volume - Half Day trips					20	150	400	400	48			1,018
Price					85	85	85	85	85			
Sales Dollars - Half Day trips	0	0	0	0	1700	12750	34000	34000	4080	0	0	86530
Sales Volume - Evening programs					20	40	50	40				150
Price					55	55	55	55				
Sales Dollars - Evening programs	0	0	0	0	1100	2200	2750	2200	0	0	0	8250
Sales Volume - Rentals					30	80	120	120	20			370
Price (average rental)					30	30	30	30	30			
Sales Dollars - Rentals	0	0	0	0	900	2400	3600	3600	600	0	0	11100
Total Sales Dollars All Products	0	0	0	0	3700	17350	40350	39800	4680	0	0	105880

These simple formulas will help you evaluate the effectiveness of your marketing projects.

FIGURE 4-5		MARKETING EVALUATION FORMULAS
Cost per Inquiry	=	Total marketing costs per marketing activity
		Total inquires resulting from marketing activity
Cost per Visitor	=	Total marketing costs per marketing activity
		Total visitors resulting from marketing activity
Return on Investment	=	Estimated visitor spending
		Total marketing costs

When calculating return on investment for marketing activities, you would look at sales generated from a specific marketing activity, for example, trips sold from a listing in your state's accommodation directory. The marketing costs are the cost of a listing in the tourism directory. Using the previous example, we assume each booked trip is worth $3,000. Your return on investment would be $30,000 (10 trips x $3,000) /$4,000 or 750 percent.

Analyzing your marketing activities this way can give you concrete information on where your business is being generated and where the best returns are occurring. One nature-based tourism operator who placed an advertisement in a national conservation publication generated over three-hundred calls for product information but very few inquiries were converted to sales. By monitoring inquiries and sales for each marketing activity, he was able to quickly assess the effectiveness of this publication for reaching his target market and generating sales.

KEY POINTS

- Active marketing is required to sell your product.
- Develop a marketing plan that looks at the product you offer, its pricing, the possible use of sales intermediaries, and the promotional activities you will use.
- Research potential customers. Group those with similar characteristics into market segments.
- Ecotourists generally prefer a variety of activities and access to remote and unique locations. Incorporating these into your product development and marketing will increase sales.
- Select marketing activities within the context of a well organized marketing plan.
- Use a well planned public relations program to get as much free publicity as possible.
- Marketing forecasts should be realistic and achievable. Early years often show low sales numbers as customer interest and loyalty develop.
- Evaluate marketing activities regularly to ensure money and efforts are well spent.

5 SUSTAINABLE TOURISM AND THE TRAVEL TRADE

YOUR RELATIONSHIP TO THE TRAVEL TRADE

As a tourism operator, you quickly become aware of the difficulties in selling your product. Marketing is a time-consuming activity to plan and often requires considerable sums of money to execute. People who are interested in your tour or lodge may not book for several years requiring you to have a large pool of customers to survive in the short term.

The travel trade can be a valuable ally. Travel wholesalers and agents have access to huge markets, understand market needs, and can sell your product to many more people than you could reach individually. This service is not inexpensive; most travel intermediaries want 30 to 40 percent of the package price as commission. You will want to be familiar with this segment of the industry and pick the most suitable organizations to sell your ecotourism product.

PLAYERS IN THE TRAVEL TRADE

The travel trade or travel services as they are sometimes called, sell or help sell the tourism product to the traveler. This sector has the ability to reach a large number of people across a large geographic region. They are:
- Wholesalers
- Tour operators
- Travel agents
- Visitors bureau
- Travel associations

Wholesalers buy up large numbers of products, such as hotel rooms, airline seats, attraction admittance's, or recreational activities. These components are packaged and either sold directly to the consumer or through another intermediary such as a travel agent or tour operator.

Tour operators deliver the actual ecotourism product but may also be a trip packager. While part of the trip may use their guides, the delivery of some of the trip may be contracted through another supplier.

Travel agents provide trip planning and booking services in exchange for a commission from the product provider. Prices for booking through a travel agent are in some cases less, as a good travel agent is able to capitalise on special rates and various travel schedules.

Visitors bureaus that function as booking agents can be an important travel intermediary. They are often the first point of contact for people planning to visit your community. In addition to the normal commission, there is sometimes a requirement for membership before they will promote your product.

Travel associations such as motor clubs also function as travel intermediaries by selling tours, accommodations, or services. The guides of the American or Canadian motor associations are used by thousands of people each year. A listing in such a guide can be very helpful in selling your product.

You will want to align your business with the organizations that most closely match your targeted customers. To create marketing opportunities, you will need to target organizations, such as destination marketing organizations, that are focused on inbound travelers for your region, or the outbound travel agents in other regions or countries that bring people to your community. Tour wholesalers and operators may deal with both inbound and outbound travelers.

THE ROLE OF THE TRAVEL TRADE IN MARKETING ECOTOURISM

The travel trade has played an important role in the tourism industry by making a large selection of products available to travelers around the world. Their role in ecotourism has been limited to a certain extent because many ecotourists choose to book their trips independently.

Join organizations that most closely match your targeted customers.

A survey done on special-interest travel buyers, which includes soft adventure, culture, nature and ecotourism tours, found that almost three-quarters of tour participants book direct. Only 25.9 percent booked through a travel agent. In the case of tourists looking for hard-adventure activities, only 13.7 percent booked through a travel agent. [1] Similar results were found in a study of North American Ecotourists by the Alberta, British Columbia, and Canadian governments (Table 5-1).

Within the travel trade there are also agencies that specialize in ecotourism and related products. These people have a better understanding of the products offered and the customers needs. A travel agent that works with more mainstream products is less likely to sell ecotourism tours, as they are not familiar with the experience or the selling points important to experienced ecotourists. A travel agent who markets a national park bus tour as a nature experience, sightseeing from a window, will not be successful in attracting ecotourists.

The importance of "a personal touch." Seventy percent of respondents chose a destination or service they had either used before or heard about from friends and colleagues.

TABLE 5-1	SOURCE OF TRAVEL INFORMATION [2]
Source of Information	**General Consumer Sample** (Percent of Respondents)
Friends	37
Personal Experience/ Been There Before	23
Books/Magazine	16
Travel Brochure	14
Travel Association/Bureau	14
Word of Mouth	10
Travel Agent	9
Television	2
Other	7

Number of Respondents 1,072

Note: Multiple responses were permitted therefore total percentages exceed 100%.

THE DIFFICULTY IN SELLING ECOTOURISM - There are several reasons why the travel trade has not been as active in selling ecotourism as it could be. Ecotourism is surrounded by misunderstanding and confusion. Describing an ecotour is more difficult than describing a golf vacation. If a travel agent has trouble explaining products or tour, it will be difficult to sell to the consumer.

Ecotourists as a market segment have different travel requirements than other travelers. An ecotourist is usually looking for a variety of activities and may be fairly sophisticated in his requirements. An avid birdwatcher wants to visit a variety of sites and view as many species or rare sightings as possible. A travel agent not familiar with the requirements of avitourists may direct them to a tour that has great scenery but mediocre birdwatching. This mismatch can lead to dissatisfaction and a loss of future bookings.

To provide the type of experience many ecotourist seek, a travel agent must be knowledgeable of the attractions and services that appeal to nature, culture, and adventure seekers. The agent must determine what activities can be undertaken in the selected country and which ground operators provide consistent high quality service. This in addition to the normal concerns with reliability, safety, and customer service.

A tour provider can help by outlining the unique products they offer and how they differ from conventional travel products. Explaining the care that has been taken to protect the environment or to deliver high quality interpretation can be helpful shortcuts for the travel agent.

Ecotourists tend to be well educated and well read, delving into magazines on their favorite sport or interest. This makes for a knowledgeable customer who expects the same or greater level of expertise from their travel agent.

Travel agents prefer packaged products - one-stop shopping and better value.

Given the range of ecotourism activities and destinations, and the pace at which companies enter and leave the business, it is difficult to stay on top of current developments. For this reason, companies targeting this market specialize in ecotourism or adventure travel instead of trying to be all things to all people. Some agents have encountered problems in supplying products to meet the demand for ecotourism. Until recently, the number of tourism operators providing ecotourism tours or services was small. Tour packages targeted at nature lovers were also limited. This has changed greatly as new companies have entered the marketplace.

Travel agents and other intermediaries often prefer packaged products because they have the advantage of one-stop shopping and provide better value. Developing a tour package takes time and money, but the benefits for you and your community can be more substantial than selling your tour or service on its own (see Chapter 6).

If you do not want to undertake tour packaging, approach travel wholesalers who may be interested in developing a package in your area or around a nature theme.

A concern of the travel trade is finding reliable suppliers of nature tourism products because they stake their reputation on the trip they sell. If a tour wholesaler needs firm departure dates and prices two years in advance when preparing brochures for travel agents, ecotourism businesses must be able to make this commitment. This is a challenge when operating in national parks and other protected areas where permits or fees are often not set until a few months before the season. This is changing somewhat as park managers become more aware of their impact on tourism providers.

Scheduling problems may still exist and can best be dealt with by developing contingency plans. Instead of promising a hike on a specific trail it is better to develop a package around types of experiences. An alpine hike is easier to deliver than a walk along a specific ridge as you may encounter trail closures or restrictions when the actual trip date arrives.

If a product does not support low-impact travel practices and does not benefit the local economy, it's not ecotourism.

ECOTOURISM OR ECO SELL? - Imitation is the sincerest form of flattery. When a product sells, competitors try to mimic the success. The green sell, or the use of nature and the environment as a tour theme, is a way of attracting customers to trips. There are a number of suppliers who have used the eco label. However, if the product is not supported with low-impact travel practices and efforts to benefits the local economy, these products are not ecotourism. To combat this problem, many people have suggested standards and certification to identify travel suppliers who deliver sustainable tourism. Industry standards are discussed in more detail in Chapter 12.

I'M A TRAVEL AGENT- HOW CAN I SELL ECOTOURISM? - Selling ecotourism is different then selling other travel products in several ways. You still need to know your markets in terms of age, gender, origin, motivations, interests, etc. Your need to match your client's interests, personality, and budget to the right product is critical as with any type of travel. What is different is your need to:

- Screen tour operators, accommodations, and transportation suppliers to assess how "green" their product is.
- Possess knowledge on the destination's ecosystems and cultures, preferably firsthand.
- Be familiar with activities you recommend, for example, sea kayaking or wildlife viewing, and the quality of the experience offered.

Given the variety of destinations and activities found on an ecotourism trip, it is understandable that travel intermediaries selling ecotourism are specialists in the field. They need to demonstrate their value to the ecotourist in order to get their business.

Technology is making it easier for the consumer to research destinations, obtain information on tourism providers, and book trips - services that in the past were provided by travel agents. The profusion of ecotourism operators who advertise through the internet would suggest that there will be more direct sales of travel products in the future. Generating sales in this environment will require travel agents to demonstrate their ability to provide unique information or services. The ecotourism provider can help the travel agent compete by increasing the agent's knowledge base on their product and their environmentally-responsible operating methods.

EVALUATING TRAVEL SUPPLIERS

It behooves a travel agent or wholesaler to develop their own screening practices to evaluate travel suppliers commitment to environmental sustainability and to community development. For specific evidence of sustainable tourism practices, you may ask:

- Can you provide written material on your environmental policies or procedures?
- How do you support conservation or environmental organizations in the area where you operate?
- Do you buy your food products locally?
- What steps have you taken to minimize energy and water usage?
- Do your vehicles meet or exceed vehicle-emission guidelines?
- What type of interpretation do you provide customers on local nature and culture?
- Do you hire local people and guides? What are their qualifications?
- Does your business have a recycling program? What items are recycled?
- What is your disposal policy at sea?
- What is your group size for tours? How do you determine this number?
- What pre-trip information do you provide to tour participants on the local habitat and culture, and on ways to be a responsible traveler?
- How often do you visit a particular site in a week? In a season?
- How do you monitor your impact on the local environment?
- What information do you provide on opportunities for tourists to support the local community after the trip?

Providers should be prepared to answer these questions and, ideally, use them to promote their operations.

There are not necessarily any right answers to these questions. Some companies may operate in a remote protected area where they are unable to set up a recycling program. Better evidence of their sustainable practices may be the purchasing of bulk items or packing out garbage for disposal.

By asking these or similar questions, you will have a clearer understanding of the travel supplier's philosophy and operating practices. Their level of commitment and approach to sustainable tourism practices will be easier to assess after discussing specific components of ecotourism. Tourism providers should be prepared to answer these questions and, ideally, should be proactive in using these answers to promote their operations to the travel intermediaries.

SUPPORTING SUSTAINABLE TOURISM: PREPARING THE CLIENT

Selling an ecotourism tour is a significant step. Even more significant is selling the second and third trips to the same traveller. Assisting your clients in getting the most out of their experience will do a lot to meet their expectations to assure customer satisfaction. For many years, we have been changing destinations to meet the needs, real or perceived, of tourists. There is growing evidence that we cannot continue to do this, and perhaps the future of tourism lies not in changing the physical environment to fit the tourist but in changing the tourist to fit the environment.

By providing information as the traveler plans their trip, they can select the trips that best match their wants and gives them time to consider how they would be willing to change their behavior. This pre-trip information is often provided by the ecotourism supplier directly but it could be distributed by the travel agent. A stronger partnership can develop between the ecotourism provider and the travel agent, as the agent can deliver more information and a greater service level to the customer. Both agent and provider benefit from a happy customer.

Pre-trip information should be an integral part of the learning experience that accompanies an ecotour.

Pre-trip information is an integral part of the learning experience that accompanies an ecotour. A travel agent can point out the difference in the size of the group, the ratio of guides to trip participants, or the access to remote locations. Information on the geography, flora and fauna, history and culture can spark interest in attractions and activities. A reading list is often appreciated as are pre-trip gatherings where people can listen to trip leaders or past participants.

Facts on trade in endangered species help people avoid purchases of products made from them. A code of ethics for travelers can be very helpful in providing guidelines on responsible tourism, as presented in Chapter 3. Providing pre-trip information and preparing your clients will help them enjoy a unique travel experience, minimize their impact on habitat and culture, and bring them back for future ecotourism experiences.

KEY POINTS

- Travel trade intermediaries can be valuable allies as they have direct access to a large number of potential customers.
- Travel agents have been limited by their lack of ecotourism product knowledge.
- Evaluate travel suppliers against environmentally-sustainable criteria. If you are a travel supplier, be proactive in highlighting how you meet environmentally-sustainable criteria.
- Products should be priced to allow for intermediary markups or commissions.
- Prepare clients for the cultural and natural environments they will be visiting. Customers will have a better experience and be less likely to negatively impact the environment.

WORKS CITED

1 Lynne Sorensen and Dave Cresson, *Market Research Special Interest Travel Buyers,* Consumer Survey Center, Inc., 1992.

2 Source: Canadian Heritage, Industry Canada, British Columbia Ministry of Small Business, Tourism and Culture, Alberta Economic Development and Tourism, Outdoor Recreation Council of British Columbia, Ecotourism- Nature/Adventure/Culture: Alberta and British Columbia Market Demand Assessment, December 1994. pp. 4-1.

6   BUILDING PARTNERSHIPS FOR SUCCESS

MARKETING PARTNERSHIPS

One quickly realizes that marketing is very important in the success of an ecotourism business. One of the most effective ways to make your marketing dollars go further is to form partnerships. By working with other businesses that are interested in the same types of customers, the cost of marketing and promotion can be shared.

A marketing partnership can create a larger presence in the marketplace than an individual operator can. Most partnerships are loosely defined groups of companies working together to sell their products. Although there are situations where legal partnerships are created, more commonly, businesses combine their products, time, and/ or money to achieve a more marketable or cost-effective venture. Common ways of building partnerships are:

- Tour packaging - the combining of several elements of a travel experience, such as accommodations, food, and recreational activities
- Cooperative marketing - partnerships among businesses and organizations for the purpose of creating joint marketing programs
- Festivals - community celebrations or festive periods that use wildlife or culture as a theme

Marketing partnerships are very powerful but take many months or years to develop.

Partnerships also provide community support for your ecotourism product. By drawing in people from many business and community sectors, you give partners direct benefit from the sale of your product.

Marketing partnerships are very powerful but take many months or years to develop, so they should be incorporated into a marketing plan along with other activities that generate business in the shorter term. As discussed in the previous chapter, developing marketing partnerships, especially tour packaging, makes your ecotourism product more attractive to the travel trade, so look at the time spent as an investment in your future.

TOUR PACKAGING

*The advantages of
tour packaging are
price and customer
convenience.*

A tour package is the combination of two or more travel elements offered at a predetermined price. These can be transportation, accommodations, food, entrance fees to parks or attractions, guide services, entertainment, etc.

The advantages of tour packaging are price and customer convenience. Packaging should give ecotourists a less expensive and more convenient holiday than if they bought each element separately, and can provide more time for pursuing special interests. The combination of greater value and more time for fun will make it easier to sell your product.

The packages can also be developed around a theme, such as hiking in several protected areas or a bird-watching trip stopping at several communities along a waterway. Package tours can bring ecotourists to a major center/hub and then provide activities and short trips that originate from the hub. This can be a great arrangement for ecotourism in remote areas where accommodations are lacking.

Another type of package appealing to ecotourism operators is a holiday that incorporates a learning component. Many universities offer learning packages on subjects from archaeology to zoology. Other organizations are starting to recognize the appeal of these packages. Yoho National Park in Canada has a learning package that provides a research experience in the park, increasing visitor knowledge about the natural history of the area and providing revenue for the park.

THE TOUR PACKAGE PROCESS

The success of your tour package depends upon the following.
- Setting package objectives
- Researching market needs
- Using your knowledge of community activities and services
- Assessing the willingness of tourism operators to partner
- Pricing the package competitively
- Planning for development time

SETTING PACKAGE OBJECTIVES - Your objectives need to be defined early so you can measure your progress and attract the correct partners. If your objective is to make "Mountaintown" the main wildlife viewing center for the region, you will need to partner with other businesses offering wildlife viewing. If you are focusing on a cultural objective, aboriginal tourism, partners will likely come from organizations involved in cultural tourism.

RESEARCHING MARKET NEEDS - You will need to do market research and understand what customers are looking for. The ecotourism market can be attracted to tour packages as long as they incorporate elements that are important to ecotourists. In many cases, this means scenery and nature, a multitude of activities occurring in nature, and interpretation of the environment. Ecotourists like flexibility, so the ability to customize itineraries is very desirable.

You will also need information on how much ecotourists are likely to spend and how they will find out about your community. If the average tourist is spending $2,500 over a two-week period, you will need to find new markets if your tour package is priced at $3,000 for a one-week tour.

How people discover your community and who influences their vacation decisions will also help you in planning your advertising strategies. If people come as a result of advertisements in regional newspapers, you will need to budget money to cover these advertising costs.

USING YOUR KNOWLEDGE OF COMMUNITY ACTIVITIES AND SERVICES - Refer back to your objectives and consider the activities and services your community has to offer. Comparing these to your objectives will help you identify the components of your package. Look for unique activities to make the package more marketable, especially if the ecotourist cannot participate in these activities without purchasing your package. An example might be access to a very environmentally-sensitive area, such as a tour of a particular cave.

Your trip package should have a theme that can be described in a dozen words or less. This will give it focus and identity as you develop the package and again when you market it.

Ecotourism businesses should avoid the pitfall of developing a tour package along the lines of traditional tourism products. Many tour packages are developed for the motorcoach industry. However, market research shows ecotourists like to travel in small groups, so it is unlikely that you would attract ecotourists to a conventional bus tour package. You will not be able to market your package through the motorcoach industry unless you become adept at taking large groups and splitting them into smaller, more manageable groups. Given their strong marketing efforts, the ecotourism industry needs to look for creative ways to work with the motorcoach companies.

Look also for hotels and transportation companies, such as airlines or railways, to join your partnership. Ecotourists will gain greater convenience and price savings. As you add components to your package, remember to keep your market research in mind. Will your customers want each day to be full with activities or will they want a less structured approach to their holiday time? Are there going to be families purchasing your package who require services that are child-friendly? If your package is targeting a senior citizen market, you may (or may not) want to reduce the pace of activities.

This step is fun, let your imagination run wild and come up with as many creative ideas as possible. One of these may be the key to developing a unique product and will command a higher price from travelers. An aboriginal group in western Canada developed a tour package for experiencing native culture. They had initially planned a package that would allow people to visit a tepee village and spend time with elders to learn about the culture and traditional ways. After brainstorming, they added a package that would enable visitors to travel with the tribe in the traditional way and actually help set up the tepee village, a special event for the community. This package would only be available once in the year and would be positioned as an upscale package with a higher price.

Once you have identified the services and attractions that you want to include, set up an itinerary for each day of the trip. By "walking through" the itinerary, you will get a feel for the experience you are developing and can tell how many components need to be priced to arrive at your overall price. Each component you add will potentially increase the attractiveness to the ecotourist but will also increase the complexity and cost. Are you getting so complex that it is nearly impossible to deliver the product? A trip itinerary may look similar to Figure 6-1.

Sample trip itinerary for a weekend birchwatching tour.

FIGURE 6-1 **TOUR PACKAGE ITINERARY**
Tour Package Theme: Weekend Birdwatching
Target Market: Casual Birdwatchers, Independent travelers
Day One:
· Tour and area orientation held at local eco-lodge · Nature walk through lodge grounds and surrounding woods · Lunch at lodge · Afternoon birding hike through local sanctuary · Shopping at local craft center that features wildlife art · Dinner at local restaurant followed by interpretative talk by ornithologist
Day Two:
· Early morning birding at lake and wetlands · Breakfast at country inn · Visit to state park and interpretative center · Picnic lunch · Afternoon spent working with bird banders in the field · Farewell dinner at eco-lodge

ASSESSING THE WILLINGNESS OF TOURISM PARTNERS TO PACKAGE - You will need to approach other tourism organizations to determine their interest in developing and marketing a tour package. You may have specific providers in mind because their product is unique or because their environmental philosophies are consistent with yours.

For some, it can be difficult to approach industry partners as it may appear to be a David-and-Goliath scenario. A large hotel chain may appear unlikely to be interested; however, even the biggest industry player is always looking for new and better ways to market. If you have an idea for an ecotour that will give hotel guests more to do in an area, chances are they will stay longer and hotel management will be very interested. When approaching possible partners look at how a partnership can benefit them. While you want to be clear on your expectations of a partnership, you also need to be clear on how everyone will win. Aim for specific benefits in your presentations. An extra 2,000 visitor days a year is a more convincing lure than the chance to make people more environmentally aware, although both are worthwhile goals.

While these businesses will take your bookings for rooms or visits to attractions, what you want is their active participation in marketing of the package. If they are willing to send out a brochure advertising your package, you will have the benefit of a combined marketing effort. To make this work all partners must be willing to promote the package with both their time and money.

PRICING THE PACKAGE COMPETITIVELY - Packaging is a successful marketing strategy because it gives the ecotourist a better value for their money then independent travel. It is critical that the package price never exceeds the retail price of the items purchased separately. This will require negotiations with your partners to determine an acceptable price for each component. In addition, determine the conditions for bookings with each company. If they require a fifty-percent deposit, you need to build this into your package booking policy or finance it yourself. Cancellation policies should also be explored and some consistency built in. To price your package, include the following elements:

· Variable costs per person
· Fixed costs per person
· Overhead and marketing costs per person
· Commissions
· Profit
· Discounts
· Refunds and credits

Variable costs are those costs that vary directly with the number of people on the tour. The room charges at your eco-lodge vary directly with the number of people. If you have six ecotourists traveling as singles, you will be charged for six rooms. Park fees, meals, and equipment rental would be also be variable costs.

Fixed costs are the costs that do not vary with the number of people on the tour. Van rental is an example, as are a guide's wages. When determining fixed costs per person, as a rule of thumb, assume you will sell 60 percent of tour capacity. If your tour accommodates 12 people, divide the van cost by 7 people (12 times 60 percent) for planning purpose. If you sell more than 7 packages, you will make money, if you sell less than 7 packages, you lose money.

The costs of marketing, booking, and purchasing for the trip must be factored in with overhead expenses. You need to estimate the share of overhead per person per trip. If you plan fifty trips a year, each tour should account for 1/50 of your annual overhead expense. Again, calculate a per person cost based of on a 60 percent tour capacity.

Commissions are an important part of selling your package through wholesalers or travel agents. Travel agents usually require a 10 percent commission. Wholesalers will also add a 35 to 45 percent markup, so it is quite possible that the tour will need to be marked up 80 to 90 percent from its cost to cover commissions and profit.

Sometimes people overlook the principle of sustainability when it comes to their business' financial health. In order for an ecotourism business to be sustainable, it must make a profit over the long term even though early years may incur losses. Profit means you have covered all your operating costs and that you are making money that can be used to replenish your capital. A profit margin for ecotourism may be in the 5 to 10 percent range, so when you take into consideration all the markups to cover advertising, commissions, and contingencies on your base cost, the selling price will be about double your land cost. (Information on financial management is provided in Chapter 7.)

For an ecotourism business to be sustainable, it must make a profit.

Price differentials and discounts affect pricing. Accommodation rates or entrance fees vary with the season. You may need to develop package prices that reflect these variances. Also consider discounts for special groups such as seniors or members of conservation groups. If you will be making a donation to a conservation group for each booking, that will need to be included. Some ecotourism market segments, such as birdwatchers, attract people in the 50-plus age group. Offering a senior discount in these cases may be expected; however, given that they may represent a significant number of tour participants, you will need to account for the discount in the price.

Once you have established your package price, compare it to similar products. Look at other package brochures and talk to your partners. Is your package priced competitively? If you have developed a unique product or are located in a remote location, you may be able to justify a higher price.

You should also plan for refunds and credits as part of a customer-satisfaction guarantee. Your management process needs to include mechanisms to ensure that each package delivers a consistent experience. However, anticipate the need for refunds or credits when severe weather or other unfavorable conditions arise. An unhappy customer is the worst form of advertising.

PLANNING DEVELOPMENT TIME - Underestimating the amount of time required to develop and market a package is common. Most packages take eighteen months to two years to develop. Tour packaging is a marketing partnership. As you increase the number of parties in the partnership, you increase the time required to move through the process. As well, you need to incorporate the business cycles of your selling agencies. If you decide to tackle the motorcoach market, you need to present a package to them two years in advance of the first visit. Likewise, wholesale travel agents need to incorporate the package into their advertising material, brochures, and catalogues, and market these to consumers. One of the challenges of the ecotourism industry is being able to commit to tour dates two years hence.

An unhappy customer is the worst form of advertising.

Some tour wholesalers have the perception that nature or cultural tourism businesses are not easily incorporated into their packages because they cannot handle large groups or cannot guarantee dates far into the future. There is some merit to this. Ecotourism, by its very underlying principles, is not mass tourism and may require partnerships among several operators to handle large groups.

There is difficulty in planning years ahead if you have not been allocated dates and permits for national parks and protected areas in advance. Government agencies are usually concerned with the upcoming year. Detailed bookings for one or two years hence may not be possible. As an alternative, you can plan tours to areas not requiring the same level of permits or advertise tours without specific departure dates and provide these as inquiries are received.

MARKETING YOUR TOUR PACKAGE

Marketing can be done through the following venues:
- Direct sales
- Retail travel agents
- Wholesale travel agents
- Local distribution

DIRECT SALES - You may find this method easiest to adopt, although the returns may not be as great. Direct sales involves printing brochures or flyers and distributing these to past customers or using qualified mailing lists to reach potential customers.

Newspaper or magazine advertisements can also be used to sell packages although costs are usually higher. The internet can be a low cost way to direct sell. The use of a company profile or advertisement on-line allows a company to reach many customers directly with minimal cost.

RETAIL TRAVEL AGENTS - Using a travel agent to distribute your brochures allows you to access a larger market. Costs can be managed more effectively as travel agents receive a commission only if the product is sold. Travel agents may not be familiar with ecotourism products or understand the experience being offered, thus hindering efforts to sell the package. Because it is commission based, your package must also compete with hundreds of other packages. (See Chapter 5 for ideas on positioning your product with travel agents.)

WHOLESALE TRAVEL AGENTS - Wholesalers can be your key to large markets and international tourists. These companies have wide-reaching marketing plans. They have an established customer base and reputation in the marketplace. They are understandably protective of their reputation and customers, and will be interested in your organization's reliability and quality control mechanisms.

Your challenge is to consistently deliver the same quality of experience even though specific components may be different.

How will your business deliver a consistent product given that you are often relying upon natural phenomena? If wolves are not sighted can you still deliver a tour experience that lives up to your theme of "northern lights and wildlife"? If you are promoting aboriginal tours, some rituals or dances may be limited to specific times of the year. Your challenge will be to consistently deliver tours that provide the same quality of experience even though specific components may be different.

Some countries in Europe and Asia have strict liability laws that protect travelers from false advertising. If you have advertised accommodations in a specific eco-lodge and, due to overbooking by the lodge, your package customers are sent to a hotel, you could face legal action for not delivering the trip as advertised in your brochures.

Marketing to wholesalers requires the same diligence as with any other customer. You need to understand their needs and package selection process. Mass mailings are often ineffective, as they receive huge quantities of mail. Some even use coded mailing labels to distinguish solicited from unsolicited mail. Direct selling by phone or in person can be used instead.

Attending trade shows for wholesalers, such as those organized by the National Tour Association (NTA) or the American Bus Association (ABA), may be one of the best ways to sell your package. There are opportunities to schedule brief meetings with wholesalers to introduce your product. Make sure you have done your homework on those wholesalers most likely to need packages in your region. Start with an organized presentation on your product, then send detailed material on trip itineraries and costs, and finally arrange familiarization tours for those people seriously interested in your product. Again, allow enough time for the marketing process. To obtain information on trade show dates and locations contact your local tourism offices or visitors' bureau.

LOCAL DISTRIBUTION - Local outlets can help distribute your brochures. Retail stores, restaurants, hotels, and attractions often have racks for tour package brochures. Community operated tourist information centres and visitor bureaus are also a good way to get your brochures in the hands of regional visitors. Your partners can also use their signage and regular marketing activities to promote your package.

COOPERATIVE MARKETING PARTNERSHIPS

Cooperative marketing is an effective way to promote your business to a larger number of people. It occurs when a number of tourism organizations join together to market a destination. They share expertise and costs so that as a group they can command a larger presence in the marketplace.

As an example, a cooperative marketing partnership may work on an advertising campaign aimed at the visiting friends and relatives (VFR) market. For this, they may develop a newspaper advertisement for regional papers that promotes a number of ecotourism activities in the area. Coupons or special rates can be successful in encouraging visitation and evaluating the advertising campaign.

Cooperative marketing partnerships share expertise and cost for greater market presence.

Other cooperative marketing partnerships may see ecotourism tour companies partner with hotels or resorts to promote a specific destination. By adding a nature experience to an accommodation, they answer the question "What do we do?" for people looking at vacation choices.

Estes Park in Colorado has been effective in developing cooperative marketing partnerships to promote their community. By highlighting the wildlife viewing experiences, they created a unique market niche for their town to attract visitors.

Cooperative mailing is a form of marketing partnership that is easy for ecotourism businesses to access. They can join with other ecotourism operators to mail brochures or news releases to target customers or media contacts. Purchasing qualified mailing lists can be quite expensive; sharing mailing lists and postage costs can be a cost-effective way to reach your target audience.

An electronic version of marketing partnerships exists on the internet, where businesses link web sites. People visiting one ecotourism web site are likely to be interested in related sites, so linking sites can increase exposure with little extra cost. Some larger sites such as visitor's bureau are now charging for links; however, the cost may be justified if it increases your site's hits.

FESTIVALS

Festivals are a unique type of tourism package. Community partners come together for a special event that highlights a unique feature of the area. For ecotourism organizations, festivals are a great way to build marketing partnerships because often the festival theme revolves around a wildlife or cultural phenomenon.

Wildlife festivals have been especially effective in attracting people to a community while promoting conservation. Communities have used wildlife migration as themes for festivals. Qualicom Beach and Parksville, British Columbia, host the Brant Geese Festival each spring as the geese migrate through. The Hummer/Bird Festival of Rockport and Fulton, Texas has grown rapidly as people come to observe these jewel-like creatures each year. Often festivals include:

Festivals are powerful vehicles for delivering economic benefits to the community.

- · Wildlife-viewing opportunities
- · Interpretative talks
- · Culinary contests (cookoffs)
- · Sporting events (for example, a 10K run for a salmon run festival)
- · Displays and sales by local artisans
- · Theatre performances
- · Dedication ceremonies
- · Children's games
- · Parades

These festivals are unique because the theme is conservation of the natural environment. Often, it is community and environmental groups that provide much of the manpower for the planning and execution of the event. Money raised from events will often be used to enhance a natural area or secure land for habitat protection.

Festivals are powerful vehicles for delivering economic benefits to the community. To the extent that the festival can attract tourists from out of the area, the community will be the recipient of additional tourism spending. The Wings Over The Platte Festival of Grand Island, Nebraska, occurs over several weekends in early spring to celebrate the return of the sandhill crane. Visitation at this festival has grown to thousands of crane-viewing days each year (a crane-viewing day is defined as each day a person spends at the festival). In 1991, the net economic benefit to the community was estimated to be $27 million. Economic benefits like this garner the attention of local decision-makers and can be a great opportunity to build partnerships.

CASE STUDY: WILDLIFE FESTIVALS GENERATE ECONOMIC BENEFITS !

Many communities have wildlife-watching festivals as a low cost way to meet the wildlife viewing demands of local people and tourists, stimulate economic activity and promote conservation. This method of attracting tourism to rural communities appears quite successful. Steve Lorton, Northwest editor for Sunset magazine, said "Watchable wildlife is big, big business. The future of tourism is going to be very dependent on it."

Some examples of wildlife viewing festivals and attractions are featured below.

1. Nanaimo, B.C., turned a local nuisance into **The Sea Lion Festival** when they created a festival around the large numbers of sea lions that gathered there in late January or February. Ten thousand people came in 1992, generating $200,000 in revenue.

2. Each April the **Brant Geese Festival** in Parksville, B.C., attracts over 2,500 people to watch the migration of 20,000 Brant geese and to participate in a variety of educational and entertainment events. The amount of money spent in the community in 1992 was $374,850.

3. **Wings Over The Platte** is held in mid-March in Grand Island, Nebraska. This wildlife and art festival revolves around the spring migration of over 500,000 Sandhill Cranes. In 1991, approximately 216,000 "crane watching days" generated over $15 million in spending for a net economic benefit of $27 million to the community.

4. The **Hawk Mountain Sanctuary** in Eastern Pennsylvania's Appalachian mountains was the first sanctuary ever established for birds of prey. Every fall, thousands of people gather at the sanctuary to watch the migration of over 24,000 raptors representing 16 species. In 1992 they had over 70,000 visitors, most of them arriving during October.

Reprinted from: Kalahari Management Inc., *Ecotourism Management*, November/December 1992.

Cultural festivals also offer opportunities to promote an ecotourism venture. Banff, Alberta has the internationally-known Festival of Mountain Films each year that presents films focusing on mountain activities and communities. While much of the action is aimed at visual arts, it has expanded to include a literary component and is a good venue for making informal contacts with adventure and travel-minded people.

It is obviously easier to get involved in an existing event than starting one from scratch.

It is obviously easier to get involved in an existing event than it is to start one from scratch. A tour operator can participate by offering tours. While the amount charged for festival tours is often minimal, it should cover costs, and is a good way to get exposure. Another way to benefit is to advertise your business during the event. The use of coupons can be effective. Providing a small discount or offering a partial reduction on multiple-person bookings during a festival can give people the feeling they are getting a special deal. Many tourism businesses have found couponing to be popular with family travellers or anyone trying to stretch their vacation dollars.

If a festival does not exist in your area and you want to create one, look for a community or conservation group that could undertake its organization. A festival is a large undertaking for any one organization, especially a business that needs to spend most of its time making money. Volunteers from chambers of commerce, conservation groups, Boy Scouts, etc. working together have the best chance of creating a successful festival. Ecotourism businesses are part of the process by donating money, supplies, or services. The best festivals have widespread community support.

KEY POINTS

- Partnerships can be the most effective way to develop and sell your product.
- Tour packages are a popular way of presenting an ecotourism experience to the traveler.
- Wildlife festivals have been valuable in attracting ecotourists to communities, often during shoulder seasons when many tourism facilities are underutilized.
- Working with other tourism businesses in cooperative marketing efforts can be an effective way of getting more visibility from limited marketing dollars.
- Do not limit you search for marketing partners to ecotourism businesses. Expand your search to all sectors of the tourism industry and potentially non-tourism organizations.

7 THE DOLLARS AND SENSE OF YOUR BUSINESS

FINANCIAL MANAGEMENT NEEDED?

You've come up with the ideal product and implemented a perfect marketing plan. Now you need to manage the finances to keep your business profitable and generate positive cash flow.

While profits for ecotourism operators as a group are relatively low, they vary somewhat by the type of activity.

At this time, many ecotourism operators are not making large sums of money. A study released by Tourism Canada in 1995 found the average adventure-travel operator had gross revenues of CDN $246,821 [1] (approximately US $180,000). Although a study on adventure travel, many companies studied offered activities such as hiking, wildlife viewing, or water activities, so these results are relevant to ecotourism. A sobering statistic from the report is that 46 percent reported annual sales of less than CDN $50,000 (approximately US $36,700). Many activities, e.g., wildlife viewing, dog sledding, sea kayaking, were seasonal in nature. Only 16 percent were year-round, so this low average figure can be rationalized to some extent as representing only a partial year's activity for most operators. On the other hand, this is a sales figure, not a profit figure, and after operating expenses, you would have a *very* modest profit.

While profits for ecotourism operators as a group are relatively low, they vary somewhat by the type of activity. The study found that gross profits for the industry as a whole averaged 18.3 percent. Nature observation, a component of many ecotourism businesses, had a higher gross profit of 27.6 percent, and many types of wildlife viewing had average profits of 18.1 percent to 18.5 percent. The highest were found in soft-adventure activities such as sea kayaking (30.7 percent), bicycling (30.1 percent), and river kayaking (25.2 percent). [2]

An encouraging trend is the growth in ecotourism products. More businesses are entering the market and more travelers are looking for ecotourism experiences. The Tourism Canada study found that travel revenues for adventure-tour operators increased 12.9 percent from 1992 to 1993. [3] Another Canadian study found there were 13.2 million potential ecotourism customers in just seven major cities in the United States and Canada. [4] Such potential should translate into increasing sales.

Because most ecotourism operators are small and medium sized businesses, it is

Every tour operator shoud have a basic business literacy to prevent fraud, avoid cash-flow problems, and maximize return on investment.

very important that financial resources are managed carefully. Low levels of sales, modest gross margins, and seasonal revenue streams create unique challenges. Add to this financing, government regulations, record keeping, and tax preparation, and you can see that the business side of your ecotourism company requires attention from skilled people or you will diminish the profits created by your hard work. What can you do to increase the financial strength of your company and minimize the time required for financial housekeeping?

It is important to be familiar with basic procedures and documents and see that they are completed. This does not mean every tour operator has to become an accountant, but every owner and manager should have a basic business literacy. Day to day functions can be delegated to staff or outside experts, but it is important to have the knowledge to prevent fraud, avoid cash-flow problems, and maximize return on investment.

FINANCIAL FORECASTING

FINANCIAL PROFORMA - If you are in a start-up situation or applying for financing, you may be asked to prepare proforma statements. You may also prepare proforma statements as part of your annual planning process. A proforma statement is the preparation of financial statements, usually a balance sheet and/or an income statement, using transactions that have not yet occurred. In effect, you are forecasting your revenue, expense, asset, and liability positions.

An example of a proforma income statement is shown in Figure 7-1. The categories shown for revenues and expenses can be modified to suit your business type but you need to ensure enough detail is used to allow an accurate forecast. Cost categories would likely vary from the examples shown depending on the type of ecotourism business. For many tour companies you would not find large inventories, perhaps only some food items or promotional items such as T-shirts. An ecotourism lodge conversely could have larger inventories of food and beverage products, plus housekeeping and maintenance items. Many ecotourism operators would receive payment for services by cash, cheque, or credit card. They would not extend credit to their customers, so would not have accounts receivable. Accounts receivable could arise if a tour operator is using a sales intermediary, such as a travel agent, and receives payment after the trip has been sold to the customer. For most companies this will not be a significant concern when managing their financial affairs.

Once you have established a format for your proforma statements, the most difficult

FIGURE 7 - 1 PROFORMA INCOME STATEMENT

KALAHARI KAYAKING - PROFORMA INCOME STATEMENT

	Jan. $	Feb. $	Mar. $	April $	May $	June $	July $	Aug. $	Sept. $	Oct. $	Nov. $	Dec. $	2008	2009	2010
Sales															
Rental					2,800	14,950	36,750	36,200	4,080				94,780	108,997	125,347
Tours				900	2,400	3,600	3,600	600					11,100	13,320	15,984
Packages													0	20,000	50,000
Commissions													0	-4,000	-10,000
Total Sales	0	0	0	0	3,700	17,350	40,350	39,800	4,680	0	0	0	105,880	138,317	181,331
Expenses															
Cost of Sales					2,220	10,410	24,210	23,880	2,808				63,528	85,057	127,816
Gross Margins	0	0	0	0	1,480	6,940	16,140	15,920	1,872	0	0	0	42,352	53,260	53,515
Accounting	100	100	100	100	100	200	200	200	100	100	100	100	1,500	1,530	1,561
Advertising	300	300	300	300	300	300	300	300	300	300	300	300	3,600	3,672	3,745
Computer supp	100	100	100	100	100	100	100	100	100	100	100	100	1,200	1,224	1,248
Loan Interest	0	167	167	167	167	167	167	167	167	167	167	167	1,833	1,600	1,200
Legal		500											500	510	520
Memberships			300										300	306	312
Office Supplies	30	30	30	30	30	30	30	30	30	30	30	30	360	367	375
Postage	50	50	50	50	50	50	50	50	50	50	50	50	600	612	624
Promotion		1,000											1,00	1,020	1,040
Rent	00	00	00	00	350	350	350	350	350	00	00	00	1,750	1,785	1,821
Salaries	2,000	2,000	2,000	2,000	2,000	2,000	2,000	2,000	2,000	2,000	2,000	2,000	24,000	24,480	24,970
Telephone	100	100	100	100	100	100	100	100	100	100	100	100	1,200	1,224	1,248
Travel													00	00	00
Total Expense	2,680	3,347	4,147	2,847	3,197	3,297	3,297	3,297	3,197	2,847	2,847	2,847	37,843	38,330	33,665
NET INCOME	-2,680	-3,347	-4,147	-2,847	-1,717	3,643	12,843	12,623	-1,325	-2,847	-2,847	-2,847	4,509	14,930	14,850

	2008	2009	2010
Net Profits to Sales	4%	11%	8%
Return on Equity	43%		

part of the proforma income statement will be generating sales figures. A detailed marketing plan will make this task easier, as you will have an idea of the volume you expect to sell and a predicted selling price. This is discussed in more detail in Chapter 4.

A proforma balance sheet would show the same asset and liability categories or accounts found on your actual balance sheet. For people unfamiliar with a balance sheet, it is a schedule which shows your business assets, liabilities incurred to buy the assets or to generate revenue, and equity in the business. A Proforma Balance Sheet is shown in Figure 7-2.

FIGURE 7-2 **PROFORMA BALANCE SHEET**	
Per month / day / year	
KALAHARI KAYAKING	
PROFORMA BALANCE SHEET	
April 30, 2008	
	$
ASSETS	
Cash	22,460
Inventory	100
Total Curent Assests	22,560
Equipment	20,000
Incorporation Costs	500
Total Assets	43,060
LIABILITIES	
Accounts Payable	4,700
Bank Laon - Current Portion	3,900
Total Current Liabilities	8,600
Bank Loans	14,000
Other Loans	10,000
Total Liabilities	32,600
SHAREHOLDER'S EQUITY	
Share Capital	100
Trained Earnings	10,360
Total Shareholders Equity	10,460
Total Liablities & Shareholders Equity	43,060

BUDGETING - Goal setting is a characteristic of successful businesses and a budget is a critical part of this process. It is a financial forecast of your operating and capital activities.

An operating budget deals with the daily running of your business. In the operating budget you forecast sales revenue and expenses. Net income gives you an indication of whether you will meet your profitability goal. Use internal data, if you have the benefit of an operating history, or research information from related fields, such as tourism forecasts for the industry or your region, to derive revenue estimates. Operating expense forecasts can be made using historical records or obtaining estimates from major suppliers.

Capital budgets is forecasting the money needed for the purchase of equipment, land, and buildings. It looks several years into the future and evaluates which purchases would be best for a company. Research to gather information on the projected costs, revenues, and cost savings is needed to evaluate the benefits of a purchase against its costs. To adequately analyze your decision on whether to buy, you would take into account the time value of money and use cash flows that have been discounted for this (basically, a dollar spent today costs more than a dollar spent a year from now). Capital budgets are normally not done by ecotourism organizations as their capital requirements are small, however, larger facilities such as lodges or attractions should prepare capital budgets and use a cost benefit analysis to guide their investment decisions. Reference books on finance concepts can provide more direction if you require a detailed capital budget.

Remember, your budget is the financial blueprint that will translate your goals into reality.

Operating and capital budgets are usually done annually. A sample operating budget worksheet is shown in Figure 7-3 and is included on the accompanying disk. With computer applications, it is relatively easy to develop a budget spreadsheet so that changes to your projections can be made easily.

When you have completed your budget, take the time to give it a reasonability test. Remember, your budget is the financial blueprint that will translate your goals into reality. To achieve your goals make sure adequate resources have been allocated. If you have established improved customer service as one of your goals, there should be corresponding budget items to accomplish this goal. Have you included money for customer service training? Are there wage costs set aside to develop a customer-tracking system to determine if you have a higher number of repeat visitors? Have you decreased marketing costs because you expect your customer service improvements to generate more word-of-mouth sales? An absence of these types of relationships between revenue, costs, and your business goals will decrease your chances of accomplishing your goals. This will also cause confusion among your staff as they detect the inconsistency between what you say you want to do and what you are actually doing.

FIGURE 7 - 3 OPERATING BUDGET

KALAHARI KAYAKING - OPERATING BUDGET

	Jan. $	Feb. $	Mar. $	April $	May $	June $	July $	Aug. $	Sept. $	Oct. $	Nov. $	Dec. $	Total 2008	Total 2009	Total 2010
Sales															
Rental					2,800	14,950	36,750	36,200	4,080				94,780	108,997	125,347
Tours					900	2,400	3,600	3,600	600				11,100	13,320	15,984
Packages													00	20,000	50,000
Total Sales	0	0	0	0	3,700	17,350	40,350	39,800	4,680	0	0	0	105,880	138,317	191,331
Expenses															
Cost of Sales					2,220	10,410	24,210	23,880	2,808				63,528	85,057	127,816
Accounting	100	100	100	100	100	200	200	200	100	100	100	100	1,500	1,530	1,561
Advertising	300	300	300	300	300	300	300	300	300	300	300	300	3,600	3,672	3,745
Computer supp	100	100	100	100	100	100	100	100	100	100	100	100	1,200	1,224	1,248
Loan Interest	0	167	167	167	167	167	167	167	167	167	167	167	1,833	1,600	1,200
Legal		500											500	510	520
Membership		300											300	306	312
Office Supplies	30	30	30	30	30	30	30	30	30	30	30	30	360	367	375
Postage	50	50	50	50	50	50	50	50	50	50	50	50	600	612	624
Promotion			1,000										1,000	1,020	1,040
Rent	00	00	00	00	350	350	350	350	350	00	00	00	1,750	1,785	1,821
Salaries	2,000	2,000	2,000	2,000	2,000	2,000	2,000	2,000	2,000	2,000	2,000	2,000	24,000	24,480	24,970
Telephone	100	100	100	100	100	100	100	100	100	100	10	100	1,200	1,224	1,248
Travel													00	00	00
Total Expense	2,680	3,180	3,980	2,680	5,250	13,540	27,340	27,010	5,838	2,680	2,680	2,680	99,538	121,330	165,281
Budgeted Income	-2,680	-3,180	-3,980	-2,680	-1,550	3,810	13,010	12,790	-1,158	-2,680	-2,680	-2,680	6,342	20,530	26,050

FIGURE 7 - 4 KALAHAARI KAYAKING

CASH FLOW FORECAST FOR THE YEAR 2008

	JAN.	FEB.	MARCH	APRIL	MAY	JUNE	JULY	AUGUST	SEPT.	OCT.	NOV.	DEC.	TOTAL
Cash On Hand	8,500	33,500	30,420	26,840	22,460	22,080	33,780	60,190	72,250	49,520	43,282	40,202	8,500
Cash Receipts:													
New Investment	10,000												10,000
Sales - Cash				3,700		17,350	40,350	39,800	4,680	000	000	000	105,880
Sales- On Account									000				
Bank Loan	15,000												15,000
Total Cash Receipts	25,000	000	000	000	3,700	17,350	40,350	39,800	4,680	000	000	000	130,880
Total Cash	33,500	33,500	30,420	26,840	26,160	39,430	74,130	99,990	76,930	49,520	43,282	40,202	139,380
Cash Disbursements:													
Operating Expenses	2,680	3,130	3,980	3,680	5,250	13,540	27,340	27,010	5,838	2,680	2,680	97,858	
Bank Loan Repayment		400	400	400	400	400	400	400	400	400	400	400	4,400
Withdrawals													000
Capital Expenditures													000
Total Cash Disbursements	000	3,080	3,580	4,380	4,080	5,650	13,940	27,740	27,410	6,238	3,080	3,080	2,258
Net Cash Flow	33,500	30,420	26,840	22,460	22,080	33,780	60,190	72,250	49,520	43,282	40,202	37,122	37,122

CASH FLOW FORECASTING - Once the budgeting process is complete, it is a good idea to do a cash flow forecast. A cash flow forecast takes the sales and expenses you forecast in the budget and looks at the timing of the money coming in and going out through your business. It alerts you to cash shortages and to investment opportunities where you have cash surpluses. This is very important with the seasonality experienced by most ecotourism operators. If you are conducting whale watching tours from February to August, you will incur most of your marketing costs prior to the season start-up. You will need financing to cover expenses until revenues come in.

A problem encountered by some small business managers is the use of their bank balance as the only cash flow forecasting tool. With a large balance in the bank account at the end of their operating season, they may make a large personal expenditure during the winter months. Unfortunately, they may not have accounted for operating expenses such as rent and repair of safety equipment required for season start-up. By making expenditures without a cash flow forecast, at the very least, they have incurred additional interest expense, and at the worst, they could jeopardized the future of their business.

A cash flow forecast is similar to an operating budget. The main difference is it looks only at cash items and the timing of cash moving in and out of the business. A copy of a cash flow worksheet is shown in Figure 7-4. For example, your proforma income statement or operating budget would show trip revenues for the months when you expect sales to occur. On the cash flow forecast you would show the sales when money is received. If you receive a deposit for a trip in March with the balance to be paid in July, you show the deposit as cash received in March (Cash In for March) and the remainder as cash received in July (Cash In for July).

By making expenditures without a cash flow forecast, you can jeopardize the future of your business.

The same principle would apply to expenditures. If you have credit with your suppliers, it is likely that you incur expenses a month before you actually pay for them. If you order brochures in December and pay a deposit in December with the balance due in January, you show cash spent in the amount of the deposit in December (Cash Out) and the balance in January (Cash Out).

Some businesses update their cash flow forecasts daily, others weekly or monthly. Frequency depends upon the activity level of your business, the season, and your access to financing. If you are in the midst of your busy season and incurring large expenditures, you might do a forecast weekly or even daily. Having a line of credit allows some breathing room with any cash shortages. If you are relying on cash inflows to cover your cash outflows, you may have to perform a delicate balancing act between payment to suppliers and receiving payments from customers. Ecotourism businesses also count on the cash surplus from one year to cover the start up expenses or capital purchases for the next operating season.

A sensitivity analysis examines the "what ifs" in your financial plan.

SENSITIVITY ANALYSIS - When completing any type of financial forecast, there is always guesswork. Based upon your experience you will estimate sales volumes and revenues. You can carefully project capital and operating expenditures. Often, though, the best laid plans go awry. A spell of bad weather can decrease sales during your peak season. A key guide may leave suddenly, requiring skilled contract help at a premium. One of your trips may receive favorable mention in a national publication and bookings increase by 200 percent.

To be sure you are prepared for these events, perform a sensitivity analysis on your forecasts of key variables. A sensitivity analysis is nothing more than a "what if" examination of the assumptions underlying your financial proformas and operating budgets. What if my sales volume is 10 percent greater than forecast? What if it is 10 percent less? Will I still generate a profit? Will I still be able to pay my bills? What if I have to decrease my prices by 5 percent to sell the number of trips targeted in my marketing plan? What if the foreign exchange rate increases dramatically and my trip becomes very expensive for a key geographic market segment?

U.S. Companies that target Canadian customers are quite aware that foreign exchange rates effect their business. When the U.S. dollar is stronger against the Canadian dollar, trip prices become more expensive. This results in lower sales for the U.S. company as Canadian travelers look for products where the Canadian currency is treated more favorably.

If you are taking your financial forecasts to a banker for financing they will often want to see some type of sensitivity analysis. Forecasting is not an exact science. Some businesses make the mistake of assuming that a 10 percent increase in sales volume will translate into a 10 percent increase in profits and therefore a sensitivity analysis is not

Bankers will often want to see a sensitivity analysis before providing financing.

needed. This is not the case, because all costs may not vary directly with sales volume. Profits may not increase by 10 percent because the additional volume may require additional staff or acquisition of new equipment to handle the demand. A simple example of a sensitivity analysis is presented below.

Assume we forecast the sale of 10,000 admissions to our natural history museum at $10 each. There is a operating cost of $6 per customer and annual administration cost of $25,000. Our net income is forecast as $15,000.

Base Case:

Total revenue	10,000 x $10	= $100,000
Operating costs	10,000 x $6	- $ 60,000
		$ 40,000
Administration		- $ 25,000
Net income		$ 15,000

Both price and volume are very sensitive to change.

We do a sensitivity analysis to see what happens if we are incorrect in our sales forecast. If the number of visitors is 9,000 instead of 10,000 our net income is calculated as:

Total revenue	9,000 x $10	= $ 90,000
Operating costs	9,000 x $6 -	$ 54,000
		$ 36,000
Administration	-	$ 25,000
Net Income		$ 11,000

We see a 27 percent decrease {($11,000 - $15,000)/$15,000} arising from a 10 percent decrease in volume!

We can then examine prices to see if they are sensitive to changes. If we price it 10 percent greater than our initial forecast we charge $11 admission instead of $10. The sensitivity analysis would show:

Total revenue	10,000 x $11	= $ 110,000
Operating costs	10,000 x $6	- $ 60,000
		$ 50,000
Administration		- $ 25,000
Net income		$ 25,000

This 10 percent price increase resulted in a 66 percent net income increase {($25,000 - $15,000/$15,000)}. As an ecotourism operator, these examples tell me that both price and volume are very sensitive to change.

As a manager, I should look for ways to maintain or increase my prices, perhaps through extra services such as pre-trip briefings, because any price increase will have a very favorable impact on the bottom line. Conversely, you would know that in a very competitive market, a small decrease in price can have a disproportionate impact on profit.

With the growth in demand for ecotourism products, tour operators are finding themselves facing greater numbers of competitors. These forecast tools help identify your vulnerabilities and can help you develop marketing strategies to combat them.

FINANCIAL ANALYSIS

Financial statements provide good information on a business' strengths and weaknesses.

Being able to read your business' financial statement is necessary to make informed decisions about future events. Will your banker lend you money? Should you offer tours next year to Annapurna? Are you able to offer a larger commission to travel agents selling your product? Your financial statement provides you good information on where your business has been and its strengths and weaknesses. It cannot tell you what will happen in the future, although it helps you to make educated guesses. However, it is only as good as the information it is based upon. It is stressful trying to make business decisions based upon suspect information. Accurate records are a must.

TOOLS TO HELP YOU BETTER UNDERSTAND YOUR BUSINESS

There are numerous ratios and analyses that can be performed on financial statements. The ratios and analyses presented here are some of the most important. They will help you assess the health of your ecotourism business and speak the same language as your banker.

COMPARATIVE ANALYSIS - A comparative analysis simply compares this year's (or month's) financial statement to last year's (or month's). Not all accounting packages prepare comparative statements; however, generally accepted accounting practices recommend that you show the current and previous accounting years on financial statements. This is helpful in spotting trends. Increases in revenue or expense items or changes in liability or asset balances tell you if your plans are coming to fruition.

COMMON SIZE ANALYSIS - This is a fancy name for a common-sense review. A common-size (or vertical analysis) looks at your revenue and expense items as a percentage of sales. Table 7-1 shows a common-size analysis for a group of adventure-tour operators. Common-size analysis is common in the hospitality industry where operating margins are very small. Rather than focusing on absolute dollars, each item is viewed as a percent of sales. These percentages can then be compared to previous periods to determine if the business is becoming more or less efficient.

Salaries and wages are a large part of a tour operator's expenditures if they use North American guides. Tracking the percentage of wages against sales will tell owners if they are using their guides effectively. Food is something that can be easily wasted or stolen. Monitoring food cost percentages will let you know if there is excessive waste. Sales depend upon money being spent on marketing programs. Keeping your marketing expenditures relative to a specified range of sales will ensure you maintain a presence in the marketplace without going overboard.

TABLE 7-1 OPERATING STATISTICS OF ADVENTURE TRAVEL OPERATORS

Expense Category	Percent of sales
Labor	26.4
Marketing	7.1
Other	48.2
Gross Profit	18.3
Total	100.0

Source: *Adventure Travel In Canada: An Overview of Products, Market and Business Potential*, Tourism Canada, February 1995.

RATIO ANALYSIS - Ratio analysis is used by investors and bankers to review the performance of your business. A ratio is simply the relationship between one number and another. By looking at key ratios, investors and bankers are able to determine if you have enough money to meet your debt obligations and whether your profitability is as good as other businesses in the industry. Owners can use the financial ratios to spot potential problems in time to take corrective action. Financial ratios you will want to review measure three main elements of your business: liquidity, profitability, and growth.

Ratio analyses can help spot problems in time to take corrective action.

RATIO ANALYSIS - LIQUIDITY - Liquidity is the ability of a business to pay its bills. Assessing liquidity focuses on the current assets and liabilities on your balance sheet. A current asset is an asset that is cash or that which can easily be turned into cash, such as

Liquidity focuses on your business' current assets and liabilities.

inventory or accounts receivable. A current liability is a debt that must be paid within the next year.

A banker considering a short-term loan to your business or a trade creditor investigating your credit position, will look primarily at working capital. Working capital is current assets minus current liabilities; it represents the ability to buy merchandise in large lots or to invest in marketing campaigns.

Another way to evaluate liquidity is to calculate the current ratio. This is expressed as current assets : current liabilities. If you have $30,000 in cash, short-term investments, and inventories, and $20,000 in accounts payable, your current ratio is $30,000:$20,000 or 1.5:1 ratio. Ideally, you would have a 2:1 current ratio to ensure you have the resources to meet debts as they came due. A ratio below 1:1 means you cannot meet your short-term debts, a ratio greater than 2:1 could mean that you are missing opportunities to invest in your business.

A related ratio is the acid-test ratio which is the same as the current ratio except it excludes inventory from current assets, as they can be difficult to convert to cash. In the previous example, if inventories were $5,000 of current assets, the acid-test ratio would be calculated as ($30,000-$5,000):$20,000 or 1.25:1 ratio. For most ecotourism businesses inventories are not significant, so the current ratio and acid-test ratio will not be significantly different.

The debt-to-equity ratio is used if you are applying for financing to determine how much additional debt your company can sustain. The debt to equity ratio is calculated as:

Debt
Equity

If you have debts of $100,000 for equipment and vans and equity of $20,000, the debt to equity ratio would be ($100,000 / $20,000) or 5 :1. This would be a high debt-to-equity ratio. A lender will want assurances that you are sharing the risk. If your company is highly leveraged with a high debt to equity ratio, it means that you are risking more of your creditors' money than your own. This is acceptable if you can make your loan payments. However, in an uncertain business environment you could lose control of your business if payments can not be made. Many banks are not comfortable with a debt-to-equity ratio greater than 3.5 to 1.

RATIO ANALYSIS - PROFITABILITY - Calculating your expenses as a percent of sales is an excellent way to track your expenditures from year to year. The first calculation is gross profit to sales (shown as a percentage). This is calculated as:

Gross Profit
Sales

Gross profit is the money left after you subtract your cost of goods sold from gross sales. Gross profit is also called gross margin. It is a good indicator of how efficiently you run the business. In our earlier sensitivity analysis, sales were $100,000 and operating costs were $60,000. The gross profit or margin ($100,000 - $60,000) is $40,000. Gross profit to sales ($40,000/$100,000 x 100) is 40 percent. This shows you have 40 percent left over from each dollar in sales to cover administration costs such as marketing, insurance, management salaries, taxes, etc. The next calculation, a very important one, is net profit to sales (shown as percentage), calculated as:

$$\frac{\text{Net Profit}}{\text{Sales}}$$

Net profit is the money left after all expenses have been subtracted. Using our earlier example, net income (net profit) is $15,000 and sales are $100,000. Net profit to sales ($15,000/$100,000 x 100) is 15 percent. The difference between this and gross profit to sales is the money required to cover your general and administrative expenses. The net profit figure can be compared against other businesses in the industry to assess your performance and to evaluate your return on investment.

Profits for adventure tour operators are generally higher than for other tour operators as a whole.

TABLE 7-2 **PROFITABILITY OF ADVENTURE TOUR OPERATORS**	
Type of Business	**Average Gross Margin (%)**
Nature Observation	27.6
Bird Watching	18.1
Whale Watching	18.5
Polar Bear Watching	7.4
Canoeing	19.4
Sea Kayaking	30.7
River Kayaking	25.2
Rafting	11.1
Hiking	6.9
Rock/Ice Climbing	12.9
Bicycling	30.1
Cross-country Skiing	4.2

Source: *Adventure Travel In Canada: An Overview*, Tourism Canada, March 1995.

It is difficult to obtain financial indicators for any one segment of the tourism industry; however, the Adventure Travel In Canada study provides some specific results on adventure-tour operators, as shown in Table 7-2. Their profits were considerably higher than for tour operators as a whole. Statistics Canada has shown that for tour wholesalers and operators as an industry, the average net profit for profitable businesses is between

*Return On
Investment
measures your
annual business
performance.*

2.1 and 3.3 percent depending upon the size of the business. [5]

If you want to attract investors to your business you will need to be familiar with the concept of return on investment (ROI). ROI can be calculated in a number of ways. Regardless of the method, you are measuring the performance of your business, the annual amount of net income (profit) generated each year from the funds invested in your company. A common way of determining ROI is to calculate the return on equity:

<u>Net Profit</u>
Owner's Equity

In our example we have $75,000 in owner equity, return on equity ($15,000/$75,000 x 100) is 20 percent. An investor would expect to receive a return greater than a risk-free investment, say a term deposit with a bank. In our example, we are generating a 20 percent return on equity, which is a good rate of return and considerably higher than earned by risk-fee investments. While this does not mean that an investor will receive a payment equal to the ROI each year, it does indicate the company is creating wealth from the investment and over time should be capable of repaying the investment.

ROI depends to some extent on the type of business you operate. Tour operators generally have low capital needs. The main requirements may be for vehicles or camping and recreation equipment. In many cases, operators rent or lease these items. Though profitability for tour operators is often low, because the net investment in the business is relatively small, the return on investment is often good. A Statistics Canada profile of Tour Wholesalers and Operators in 1993 found the net profit to equity, a measure of return on investment was 38.8 percent. [6]

RATIO ANALYSIS - GROWTH - With good planning, your business will grow. One of the fastest ways to determine how well your business is growing is to calculate the growth ratios for sales, profits, assets, and debts. To illustrate the following points we will use our earlier example.

Sales growth = <u>(Sales this year - Sales last year)</u>
Sales last year

Sales were $95,000 last year. Our sales growth (($100,000-$95,000)/$95,000 x 100) is 5 percent.

Profit growth = (Profit this year - Profit last year)
                         Profit last year

Profits were $14,000 last year. Our profit growth (($15,000 - $14,000)/$14,000 x 100) is 7 percent.

Asset growth = (Assets this year - Assets last year)
                        Assets last year

Assets are $100,000 this year and $97,000 last year. Our assets growth ($100,000 - $97,000)/$97,000 x 100) is 3 percent.

Debt growth = (Total debt this year - Total debt last year)
                      Total debt last year

Debt is $25,000 this year and $30,000 last year. Our debt growth ($25,000 - $30,000)/ $30,000 x 100) is a negative 17 percent, indicating a decrease of 17 percent.

In general, a business would like to see similar growth in all four areas. If you had a five percent increase in sales but a 1 percent increase in profits, this would indicate a positive trend in sales but could mean that you have become less efficient. Unless there are start-up, marketing, or operating expenditures required to generate additional sales, you want sales and profits to grow equally.

Debt may grow as well as assets or sales, but you do not want to see debt growing more than assets. This could indicate that you are using debt to finance operating expenses.

A break-even analysis shows you at what point your business makes money.

BREAK-EVEN ANALYSIS - If you are seeking financing or trying to decide about adding a new product, you will need to perform a break-even analysis. The purpose of completing a break-even analysis is to determine at what point your business makes money. Often start-up or small businesses will look at their bank balance to tell them if they are making money. If there is money in the bank, they assume they are making money; if there is no money in the bank, they assume they are losing money. As a rough guide, these observations are not totally invalid; however, there is a difference between cash-flow (money in the bank) and profitability (the excess of revenues over expenses). If your business is growing rapidly or if you have used funds to finance capital expenditures, you may have a cash shortage but still be very profitable. Analyzing your financial statements and performing a break-even analysis gives you a better understanding of the economics of your business so you can make the right decisions at

the right time. A break even analysis provides you with information on the:
- Point at which you start to make a profit
- Incremental profits you generate with each sale or sales dollar

Variable costs fluctuate directly with the production of your product or service.

Calculating a break-even point is relatively easy; however, you will need to collect the data used in the analysis: sales, variable costs, and fixed costs. Sales figures come from your sales ledgers or proformas and should be your net sales after any refunds.

Variable costs are those costs that fluctuate directly with production of your product or delivery of your service, and ultimately, sales. If you provide overnight hiking trips, costs that vary with the number of participants are food, park fees, guide or camp staff wages, equipment rental, and printing costs of pre-trip orientation packages. In each of these cases, the costs vary directly with the number of trips sold.

Fixed costs are tied to overall increases or decreases in business activity.

Fixed costs are costs that do not vary directly with the number of trips sold such as marketing costs, management salaries, and building rent. These types of costs are tied to increases or decreases in overall business activity but they do not vary by trip. While you may need to spend much more on marketing if your business is to double in size, there is not a direct relationship between marketing costs and individual trips.

Your listing in a tourism directory will cost the same whether you offer ten trips a year or twelve. Brochures are printed for an entire season's trips and cannot be tied directly to one trip. Some individual costs, such as newspaper advertisements or special promotions, may be directly related to a particular trip but for the most part, these are treated as fixed for the purposes of doing a break-even analysis.

There are two ways to calculate your break-even point. If you have information on a per unit basis, you can calculate a break-even point for each product. More often however, tour operators have information in a broad account or cost category that lends itself to calculating a break-even point expressed in sales dollars. Either method generates the same answer, so select the method that works best for you.

The first method is to calculate the break-even point in units. Use this only if you have cost information for each trip. The formula is:

1. Contribution per unit   =   Selling price - Variable cost per unit
2. Break-even point in units = $\dfrac{\text{Fixed costs}}{\text{Contribution per unit}}$

If you operate a natural history tour company and charge customers $99 for a one-day geological tour, you could calculate the break-even point using the above formula if you knew what your costs were for the trip. You may decide that the cost of lunch, van rental, and guide services are variable costs because the costs would not be incurred if the tour was not held. These costs are estimated at $45 per person. Fixed costs would be marketing costs such as brochures and postage, office rent, telephone, insurance, and a manager's salary. Fixed costs are estimated at $40,000 per year.

The break-even point in units is calculated as:

1. Contribution per unit   =   Selling price ($99)
          -    Variable cost per unit ($45)
          = $ 54

2. Break-even point in units =   Fixed costs ($40,000)
                            Contribution per unit ($54)
          =   740.74 units or day trips
(rounded up to 741 trips because you cannot sell part of a trip)

This shows you need to sell 741 trips to break even. When you sell the 742nd trip, you have covered your fixed costs and are earning your first profits. *Please note that each unit sold after the break-even point does not generate $99 in profit but $54, as each sale has a variable cost of $45, a point often overlooked by business owners.*

What do you do if you do not know your costs by trip participant? This is often the case where businesses track expenses by category or type of trip as opposed to specific trips. In this situation use the second method to calculate a break-even point in dollars:

1. Variable cost per sales dollar = Variable costs
                                         Sales

2. Contribution per sales dollar = $1.00 - Variable cost per sales dollar

3. Break-even point   = Fixed costs
                               Contribution per sales dollar

Your estimated sales for the year are $98,000 and the estimated variable costs for van rentals, food, and contract guide services are $45,000. The remaining costs for marketing, management salaries, rent, and insurance are classified as fixed costs and are estimated to be $40,000. The break-even point would then be calculated as:

1. Variable cost per sales dollar = Variable costs ($45,000) = $ .46
                                      Sales ($98,000)

2. Contribution per sales dollar   = $1.00

           - <u>Variable Cost per sales dollar ($.46)</u>

         = $ .54

3. Break even point   =   <u>Fixed Costs ($40,000)</u>

           Contribution per sales dollar ($.54)

         = $74,074

In this example, forty six cents of each sales dollar would be needed to cover variable costs. Fifty-four cents would be available from each sales dollar to cover fixed costs. The business would break even where the contribution from each sales dollar has covered the fixed costs of $40,000. This occurs when sales reach $74,074. From this point on, each sales dollar will generate fifty-four cents in profit. As this business is forecasting $98,000 in sales ($23,926 greater than $74,074), it will reach its break-even point.

This is a very simple example of a break-even analysis. When completing such an analysis for your business you may encounter some problems classifying costs as fixed or variable. You may have salaries for guides which are paid only if a tour is offered. Here the salaries are a variable cost. However, if the salaries represent payments to owners not tied directly to the number of tours offered, these are fixed costs for the break-even analysis. Where it is difficult to classify costs, it is best to err on the side of caution and classify it as a fixed cost. This will give you a higher break-even point, but if you are budgeting for the upcoming year or for a new program, planning for a higher break-even point will give you an extra cushion if things go wrong.

OBTAINING FINANCING

Overall, banks are not familiar with the tourism and recreation industries - a sound business plan is a necessity.

Ecotourism is attractive to many would-be business owners and community planners because of the relatively small amount of capital needed for start-up. This is a good thing because obtaining financing from conventional sources is not easy for ecotourism operators. The tourism and recreation industries are not familiar to banks, and in many cases, are not regarded as good risks. Part of this is due to the instability inherent in the industry or the lack of assets for collateral, but some of the skepticism arises from the lack of preparation by business owners. A sound business plan is a necessity along with some collateral and the character to sell yourself. Banks will be looking at your background and how the debt will be repaid. You must demonstrate some experience in the ecotourism industry and management skills. Banks will also need some assurance that you are willing to invest some of your own money in the business.

Assuming you can convince a bank to lend you money, you should be concerned with the cost of the debt. Do you have the cash flow to cover the interest cost of a large bank loan? If you are hoping a bank will provide a large portion of your start-up and capital needs, be aware that a bank may want you to contribute fifty percent or more of the total needed funds before approving the loan.

For this reason, you will likely be faced with a search for sources of financing outside of a bank. What are your alternatives? As a start, you will need to consider personal assets. You will need money to support yourself until your business is established. You are also the person with the most to gain from the business. Any investor or creditor will expect to see financial contribution from you as a measure of your commitment and to ensure that you are sharing the risk. Your personal savings have the advantage of being the most flexible of funds. They do not require a repayment schedule and do not dilute the control of your business.

Another source of financing is family and friends who will lend you money because of their relationship with you. They may loan you money outright or take an ownership interest in exchange for their investment. Be sure to spell out what the expectations are on both sides. Agree on what level of control your investors will have and the terms under which money will be repaid. Again, a business plan can help in these matters.

Some regions have "seed" money available from government programs to start small businesses. These may be easier to access and have better repayment terms than conventional sources. In parts of British Columbia, money is set aside from stumpage fees in the logging industry to help establish alternative industries such as ecotourism. Contact your economic development authority or tourism agencies to see what programs may be available. These programs change frequently and may often have considerable amount of paperwork associated with them, so do your homework carefully. Some businesses find them more trouble than help.

Remember that you will likely need more money than you anticipate. Preparing a business plan will help you to anticipate these contingencies. Financing is difficult, so focus initially on minimizing your operating costs and in obtaining funds from personal resources, family, and friends. One ecotourism tour operator invested US $50,000 of his own money along with US $150,000 in lost wages to establish his business. Do not underestimate the financing you will require. Many businesses fail not because they are short on ideas but because they are short on cash.

Be prepared to invest some of your own money initially.

You will likely need more money than you anticipate.

ACCOUNTING

BOOKKEEPING - Most entrepreneurs have great ideas and a desire to make things happen. The need to track expenditures and revenues in great detail may seem pointless and not a lot of fun. However, to make their business successful and stay out of trouble with the government, it is critical to have a well functioning accounting system.

Your accounting system does not have to be expensive or elaborate. However, it is imperative that all items are recorded and charged to the correct account. With the availability of computers, many businesses will opt for a computerized accounting package. There are many software packages on the market, from very simple to very elaborate. If you do not have a computer, you can set up a basic bookkeeping system using manual records available at most stationary supply stores. Start with a Sales Ledger to record your bookings and use a Disbursement Journal to keep track of expenses. Use preprinted cash receipts with carbon paper to confirm payments by customers.

Not hiring an accountant can be one of the most expensive decisions you make when you start your business.

One thing often overlooked is the need for skilled help in accounting. You may use a friend or relative who has some bookkeeping experience, thinking a professional accountant is too expensive or an unnecessary expenditure. Nothing could be farther from the truth. Not hiring an accountant can be one of the most expensive decisions you make. At the very least you need to meet with an accountant when setting up your business to establish a chart of accounts, discuss business structure, and basic tax planning.

There are many deductions that may be overlooked or taken incorrectly because the tour operator is not familiar with tax laws. If you have family members involved in the business, there may be opportunities to take advantage of income splitting. Given that many ecotourism operators are small to medium sized businesses, they can especially benefit from sheltering as much income as possible.

Another reason for getting professional assistance is to ensure that your records are accurate. By analyzing your financial records as discussed earlier, you can determine the most profitable tours or products. To do this, you need accurate financial information. If you record the new van as a trip expense instead of a capital equipment purchase, you will find your net income unusually low and may overprice products based upon this erroneous accounting. Also, make sure to separate any personal expenditures and income from the company's to ensure accurate financial records.

PAYROLL - As your business grows, the number of people working for you will increase. Many ecotourism operators start out doing many business functions themselves and quickly find the need for additional guides, camp staff, or sales people. Payroll accounting for hourly workers is time consuming and comes with numerous regulations surrounding deductions, taxes, and wages.

A cost-effective way to maximize your time is to contract out payroll accounting as early as possible. Contact firms who specialize in payroll services. Usually they charge a small fee to setup each employee's account and then a modest fee for each pay period. For example, a payroll service provider might charge US $15 plus $1 per employee for each pay period to prepare the paychecks and make government remittances. They may also include a year-end report as part of the regular fee. Even large companies are contracting out payroll because the task is time consuming and expensive to maintain in-house expertise. Use the time saved on marketing your latest Bighorn Sheep viewing trip. You will be more successful in the long run.

TAXES - No one likes to pay taxes; however, collecting, recording, and remitting taxes is part of being a business owner. As mentioned earlier, keeping good records and doing tax planning can minimize the amount of income tax paid. It is also important to set up procedures to collect and remit sales tax, if required. Tax rates vary between and within countries. Your accountant can provide information on tax rates and a list of items that are taxable. If you are doing business in other countries, you also need to become familiar with those tax rates and collection requirements. Make sure all required tax payments to the government are made on time. Assessed penalties are an unnecessary expense.

Make sure you have a system to meet your legal obligations. Do not forget to include these costs when developing financial forecasts and pricing structures. As a business expenditure, you need to recover this cost to be profitable. Enlisting experienced help in setting up your accounting systems will help minimize the administrative burden and keep you competitive.

INTERNAL CONTROLS - As an owner or manager, one of your obligations is to protect the company from waste, fraud, and inefficiency. Internal controls are the safeguards needed to meet that obligation. Larger operators have numerous controls and audits to ensure company's assets are not being misused, lost, or stolen. Smaller operators may not have an elaborate system of internal controls but some basic controls are required nonetheless.

If you are the only person working in the business, most of the controls are aimed at ensuring the accuracy of the financial records. Providing a receipt for each sale and keeping invoices for cash expenditures are examples of internal controls.

No one wants to think their employees may be dishonest, however, when there is cash or assets that are easily consumed, theft and fraud increase. Businesses that accept cash payments or have food service operations are at a greater risk of theft or fraud.

Businesses that accept cash payments or have food service operations are at a greater risk of theft or fraud.

Simple measures to protect your business start with hiring the right people and checking references. Make sure no one employee handles a transaction from beginning to end. If one of your guides is also marketing tours and receiving the mail, have another employee make bank deposits and record revenues. By comparing the sales ledger against the tour roster, you can make sure all payments have been deposited.

Set policies on who can order materials and who can select stops for tours. You will want to use specific suppliers to maximize discounts and to avoid problems of employee collusion. Companies will offer rewards, either in cash or in-kind merchandise, for bringing customers to their business. Guides may be promised free meals for bringing a group to their restaurant. Car rental agencies may tip lodge staff who recommend them. While you may not discourage these practices, you should be aware of them. You do not want your tour groups diverted to restaurants or shops solely because of deals offered to your staff. Ecotourists are savvy travelers and will detect a compromise in quality or a feeling of being funneled into a business for someone else's benefit.

As well, prepare a budget and review your monthly or financial statements against it. This simple step can be one of the best internal controls you can implement. Even a rudimentary budget will give you some idea of what to expect for the coming year. One business owner discovered to her chagrin that an employee had been keeping the money when customers paid cash for lessons. Over a period of months the amount was substantial and was only discovered when there was not enough money to cover basic expenses, even though sales had been strong. This could have been avoided by comparing financial results against a budget. Reviewing sales forecasts would have shown that the number of lessons recorded was less than expected even though expenses were consistent with higher levels of activity. Quicker investigation could have reduced the amount of money lost.

CASH MANAGEMENT

In the earlier section on financial forecasting, the need for a cash forecast schedule was discussed. In addition to preparing this schedule, you need to spend time to regulate the amount and timing of cash coming and going through your business. This function is called cash management. It involves those activities such as cost controls that reduce cash outflows, and activities like deposit collection that increase cash inflows.

In a start-up situation your business will invariably cost more than expected and sales will be slower than expected. Some tourism operators say it took five years or more before they broke even. Cathy Pope of Mountain River Outfitters in the Canadian Northwest Territories, reported that after six years their business broke even although they were not taking wages out of the company, preferring to reinvest the money in equipment. Making sure you are around to reach your break-even point will require careful cash-management strategies. Often that means having more capital than you think you need and reducing operating costs wherever possible. Some of the most relevant cash management strategies are:

- Leasing or renting equipment instead of buying
- Contracting out services
- Minimizing operating costs
- Implementing booking deposits and cancellation fees

A budget and monthly financial review is one of the best internal controls you can implement.

Ensuring the safety of your customers is a critical marketing and operating feature, and will require good equipment and trained personnel. This does not mean you have to buy all the required equipment or hire the employees needed. The following sections look at ways to meet customer needs while practicing good cash management.

EQUIPMENT ACQUISITIONS - Equipment can often be rented or leased, although in a remote location, the range of rental options may be less. Recreation equipment is available at reasonable costs from outdoor recreation programs at many universities or colleges or from retailers who rent outdoor equipment. Vehicles and airplanes can be rented or leased, especially if usage is intermittent. If you need a meeting place from which to start your tours or make bookings, you can link up with another business so that you are not paying the full cost of an office. Canadian Wilderness Nature Guides in Waterton Park joined with Kilmorey Lodge to the benefit of both parties. Canadian Wilderness Nature Guides uses the lodge as the base for its tours and programs. Lodge guests can partake of nature programs in the lounge or read about local flora and fauna sightings on bulletin boards maintained in the lobby.

CONTRACTING OUT SERVICES - Because labor costs are significant, it may be wise to contract out some services instead of hiring employees. A contract situation enables you to bring in skilled guides without the administrative costs associated with maintaining employees. It is important, however, to ensure that you are not violating labor or tax laws by classifying someone as a contractor when they should be considered an employee.

COST MINIMIZATION - Minimizing all operating costs is important to your survival. Examine the way you market. Can you use a facsimile list to advertise your tours instead of mailing brochures? Is an internet site less expensive than producing costly brochures or multimedia presentations? Can you use e-mail to communicate with customers and suppliers to reduce phone charges? Technology can allow even the smallest of companies to expand its reach while lowering costs. Be creative and talk to other businesses about ways to work together.

DEPOSITS AND CANCELLATION FEES - An important part of your cash management is ensuring money received from customers is more than money paid to suppliers. One way to accomplish this is to ask for deposits at the time of booking and payment of the balance prior to the tour date. This approach will provide you with money to cover the expenses incurred preparing for the tour.

The amount of deposit varies with the length of the tour; tours of shorter duration may ask for a 50 percent deposit while longer, more expensive trips may ask for a deposit of several hundred dollars with payments at subsequent dates. Determine what your financial obligations will be and set the deposit policy to cover as many expenses as possible. You also need protection from people who sign up for a trip then withdraw shortly before the tour date. In many cases, you will have spent money that cannot be retrieved. A cancellation policy will help transfer those costs from yourself to the customer.

Establish a cancellation policy and communicate it to your customers.

Cancellation policies are set so a certain amount of notice is required to receive a full refund. Again depending upon the length and nature of a trip, this can vary from a week to several months. Often there is a sliding scale where less and less of the trip fee is refunded as the cancellation date moves closer to the departure date. Even in cases of "full" refunds, there is often a handling fee to cover administration costs.

Travelers are able to buy cancellation insurance that protects them from losing money due to illness or accident, and should be encouraged to do so. Not developing a cancellation policy and communicating it to your customers can lead to problems. If people do not arrive for the tour, your company will have spent money in preparation for their participation. They may demand refunds which you cannot refuse due to the lack of a clear cancellation policy.

With cancellation fees and deposits it is important to check with suppliers to see what their policies are. If you are able to cancel your commitments relatively easily you may want to pass that along to your customer. If your suppliers require long lead times for cancellations or pay significant cancellation penalties, you need to build that into your policies or you will end up paying the difference from your profits. The better way of managing cash flow is to match your cancellation and deposit policies to your suppliers and competitors.

KEY POINTS

- Ecotourism businesses often face short operating seasons, small group sizes, and low capacity utilization. Under these conditions sound financial management is critical.
- Planning for the seasonal operations most ecotourism organizations face, requires good cash management.
- Ecotourism businesses in a start-up phase may require several years to establish a clientele.
- Financing from conventional sources can be difficult to obtain for ecotourism operators. Approaching non-conventional resources such as friends or family may be a better option.
- Maintaining proper records is required for legal and tax reasons but is also important to provide good cost information for owners and managers.

WORKS CITED

1 Tourism Canada, *Adventure Travel in Canada: An Overview of Product, Market and Business Potential*, February 1995.

2 Ibid.

3 Ibid.

4 Canadian Heritage, Industry Canada, British Columbia Ministry of Small Business, Tourism and Culture, Alberta Economic Development and Tourism, Outdoor Recreation Council of British Columbia, *Ecotourism- Nature/Adventure/Culture: Alberta and British Columbia Market Demand Assessment*, December 1994.

5 Statistics Canada, Small Business and Special Surveys Division., *1993 Small Business Profiles (Canada)*, August 1995.

6 Ibid.

8 CLIMBING THE CUSTOMER SERVICE MOUNTAIN

WHAT IS CUSTOMER SERVICE?

Customer service is the ability to meet your customer's real and perceived needs through the actions of your staff and suppliers. Customer service occurs every time ecotourists come into contact with your business. It is the way they are treated whether they are calling for trip information or to make a booking. It is the impression they receive when they drive into your parking lot. It is the experience they have when they take one of your guided nature walks.

Unless you personally take care of every tour detail, assuming you are exceptional at customer service, you will have to develop a customer-service system that ensures visitors will enjoy a consistent level of customer service. The reach of customer service throughout your organization makes it one of the biggest challenges for an owner or manager.

As mentioned in Chapter 4, a business will have a very difficult time competing on price alone, and a somewhat difficult time competing on quality. Where a business can really distinguish itself is on its ability to deliver *great* customer service.

In addition to basic customer service, as in taking reservations or in food preparation and delivery, an ecotourism business has to provide interpretation, demonstration of environmental and cultural sensitivity, and a high level of safety management.

Customer service is like making love to a gorilla. You do not quit when you are satisfied, you quit when the gorilla is satisfied.

When you develop your customer service strategy, you need to refer to your market research to determine what your customers expect. You will also want to consider where you have positioned your product. If you are offering a premium product, your customers will likely expect a higher level of service. Keep in mind that customer expectations and perceptions are everything. You may feel you provide great customer service, but if your customer feels you are lacking in some area, you will lose business if others are able to meet that need. A rather profound statement seen on one business bulletin board sums it up well, "Customer service is like making love to a gorilla. You do not quit when you are satisfied, you quit when the gorilla is satisfied."

DELIVERING EXCEPTIONAL CUSTOMER SERVICE

You cannot issue an edict saying that you have great customer service and then expect it to come true. You must plan for it through a series of management actions. The success of customer service will depend to a great extent, on the following elements:

- Policies
- Procedures
- Standards
- Recruiting the right staff
- Training
- Controls
- Recognition

Lets look at each of these individually to assess your business' customer service framework.

Policies give direction.

POLICIES - Setting customer service policy helps you define the level of customer service. Policies are broad, guiding principles. They range from hiring standards to contingencies to dress code and beyond.

A policy that says you provide guides with the highest level of skill or knowledge may result in a different level of service than a policy that says you will employ people with a specific license or diploma. One nature-based tour company employs only graduates from forestry technology programs. This policy gives their tour a strong focus on forest ecology and in the process, distinguishes them from other companies.

Policies give direction to staff on what is expected of them. A policy that empowers a guide to adapt to changes will ensure customers have a fun and safe trip. A guide caught in unusually bad weather can decide to substitute a restaurant meal for a picnic lunch, knowing that he has the authority to do so.

Procedures ensure consistency.

PROCEDURES - No one likes procedures, and often they are loosely defined for small businesses, but they are important to ensure consistency. Your big challenge is not in delivering a great tour the first time, it is in delivering that great tour the one hundredth time. A simple procedure list can go a long way to communicate what good service is. When a group meets for a tour, your customer service procedure for a guide might include the following steps.

- Welcome the people to the tour.
- Have the guide introduce himself.
- Have tour members introduce themselves.

- Describe the trip, when and where there will be breaks, and when the group will return from the trip.
- Make sure everyone has the right equipment.
- Brief everyone on correct behavior for viewing wildlife, interacting with locals, and moving through sensitive environments.

Note - Do not forget office procedures. The number of times your phone rings before it is answered and the greeting used, may determine whether you get the booking in the first place.

Standards
further define what
is expected.

STANDARDS - Customer service standards are closely related to procedures, and further define what is expected from the service process. In conventional tourism products standards may include the number of meals served by a food and beverage server in one shift. For an ecotourism business, these standards may not be relevant. However, there are other standards that apply.

One standard often used is the guide-to-client ratio. Some ecotourism operations may have one guide for 12 people or more. High-end operations may have one guide for every three or four people. Obviously this standard will significantly affect your service delivery. A low guide-to-client ratio offers more flexibility in tour activities. People will have more opportunity to ask questions and learn about the environment. Other standards that may be relevant are:

- Length of time to respond to an inquiry for trip information
- Percentage of time people spend engaged in core activity (birdwatching) versus non-core activities (travel or client pickup)
- Number of contacts before and after a trip to properly brief the client
- Amount of time spent viewing a wildlife species at one time or from one location

RECRUITING - The guide is the company representative with whom customers spend the most time. It will be the stories of your guide that will be retold back home and may serve as the most vivid memories of your ecotourism product. Selecting the right person as your guide is critical. While it is easy to hire on the basis of formal qualifications, you must also take into account softer attributes, like leadership ability and communication skills. You can train people to perform a technical skill such as kayaking or historic interpretation, but you cannot teach someone how to smile. This issue is explored in more detail in Chapter 9.

TRAINING - By hiring qualified people you can minimize training requirements, but you will still want to provide basic appropriate training. Staff need to be familiar with your way of doing things. If there is a deficiency in the employee's skill set, you need to provide training to develop that skill. You will also want to keep your staff up to date in their areas of expertise and make sure people are informed about the latest developments in the areas you operate. Ensuring consistency of procedures through ongoing training and reinforcement provides protection against lawsuits if a tour goes wrong.

To plan your training activities, start by evaluating your staff training needs. Look at areas such as technical or specialty skills, contingency planning, communications, and internal procedures. Consider short-term needs, but also include a continuing education component so there is long-term improvement in skill and knowledge.

Selecting and training the right person is critical.

From your needs assessment you can then develop a training program for each person, including yourself. It can take months to finish this training, so it is important to complete the elements that are most critical first. A side benefit from this process is that, if questioned by customers or staff about employee training, you can demonstrate a logical process to identify and address training needs.

Training can be delivered in many ways. It may be on-the-job with an experienced person training a less experienced person, or it can be in the form of seminars or courses held in-house or off-site. Local colleges or technical schools often have courses that are relevant, such as guiding, first aid, customer service, and marketing. Some institutions offer courses by correspondence or rent videos for in-house training. Asking experienced staff or outside experts to speak at staff meetings can be a way to include training in your ongoing operations at a very low cost. You may also want to bring in guest trainers at the beginning of the season to do a concentrated amount of training quickly.

When you do training on-the-job, make sure you select the best person as the trainer. It will not necessarily be the person with the most experience but the person with some patience and the best way of explaining techniques. You do not want someone who is always circumventing your policies or procedures to be training your new staff, or you will end up with a team of people delivering your customer service in a manner you had not intended. Where commitment to environmental sensitivity is a business foundation, the transfer of values through policies and procedures is very important.

Controls and staff recognition encourage repeat performance of exceptional customer service.

CONTROLS - No one wants to be the watchdog for customer service, but someone must ensure quality service is delivered. Controls give you some comfort that a desired level of customer service is being delivered. Preparing job descriptions and defining your requirements for hiring are two simple, but effective, controls. Ensuring everyone receives basic training is another. A further control may have you, or a senior member of the team, participating in trips from time to time to see that guides follow procedures and are interacting with a group in a professional and competent manner. Some companies use people unknown to the guides to take tours and assess the level of customer service. The key here is to ensure a timely feedback loop to staff on their performance, both good and bad.

RECOGNITION - One of the most powerful things you can do is recognize exceptional customer service when it happens. We may explain to our staff what levels of customer service we expect and we may provide training, but if there is no follow-up, your level of customer service will be inconsistent. Using intangible or low-cost rewards to recognize the efforts of staff who go the extra mile for customers will encourage people to repeat the effort. A verbal thank you, a humorous certificate, or the opportunity to lead choice tours, will show staff that you appreciate their efforts to make your business more successful.

CUSTOMER SERVICE PROBLEMS

If you follow the steps in the previous section, you will be well-on-the-way to providing good customer service. If you have already implemented the customer-service process and are still receiving complaints, they can often be traced to one of the following problems:
- Owner or managers did not start with a clear vision of customer service.
- Owner or managers started with a clear customer-service vision but did not turn that into easy-to-understand and measurable performance standards.
- Owner or managers have rewarded employees for doing something other than what they said was good customer service.

A lack of clear performance standards is one of the biggest reasons why customer service fails.

If you do not have a clear vision of customer service you will not be able to develop good policies, procedures, or standards. You will have a hard time deciding on what training is required and what performance to reward when it occurs. One way to avoid this is to develop a written vision statement on what you are trying to deliver for customer service and how it will be provided. You may want to look at the products of other ecotourism operators. Think about what makes them attractive and incorporate those elements in your operation. Did they include a video in their pre-trip information? Were there more guides than you had planned to use? Seeing specific evidence of good service may make it easier for you to formulate your own expectations.

If you have a clear vision of customer service but are having problems delivering it, look at the next problem, a lack of clear performance standards. To be effective, you need standards that state specifically what good customer service means. Some things may seem obvious, but if you are dealing with more than one employee, i.e. yourself, you will need to make others understand what is expected of them. A guide arriving before tour participants at the staging point may seem a fairly obvious customer-service behavior, but other people's perception of time or organizational skills may result in guides arriving late. Some organizations specify that a guide will arrive fifteen minutes before trip start time to finalize arrangements and welcome early arrivals.

A lack of clear performance standards (see Figure 8-1) is one of the biggest reasons why customer service fails. Establish standards and ensure your staff are aware of them. If you do not monitor their efforts, your customer-service delivery will be inconsistent.

In the final weeks of your season, after many challenging guests and the same

---

Examples of customer service standards relevant to ecotourism businesses.

FIGURE 8-1
EXAMPLES OF CUSTOMER SERVICE PERFORMANCE STANDARDS

1. All tour participants will be greeted within five minutes of arrival.
2. Operation of trip equipment will be explained and demonstrated to all group members.
3. No trip members will be left behind. A guide will stay with slower participants or the group will slow its progress to allow the slowest members to keep up.
4. Customers will be asked about their special dietary requirements and trip cooks will incorporate these requirements into menu planning.
5. Each customer will be thanked for choosing your tour company and information on your frequent booking program will be provided.

---

interpretative talk given many, many times, it is easy to let customer service slide. Your guides may be tired, their sense of humor stretched thin, and if they think no one appreciates their efforts to make the last trip as good as the first, human nature is to let the standards relax. Let employees know you understand the demands of the job and appreciate the effort they put in. They will work harder for you.

Be creative in your recognition; a small gift or verbal pat on the back is great, but look for other ways to recognize employees. Can you give out a gift or certificate which captures a special moment or a spectacular end-of-the-season party to recognize their hard work during the season? Many ecotourism businesses employ highly trained and educated people. Do not assume because you have such people they do not need recognition. Everyone appreciates acknowledgment; it goes a long way to developing a loyal and high-performing workforce.

INTERPRETATION

Your interpretative programs should not be static. Work in new elements as conditions change.

While the primary attraction for an ecotourist is the nature or scenery found in an area, interpretation of the environment contributes greatly to their enjoyment of a tour. A study done by Forestry Tasmania on nature-based tourism found that ecotourism operators valued interpretation less than their customers. As a result, many interpretative experiences were underdeveloped and poorly marketed. [1]

Interpretation serves two primary roles; one, it encourages interaction between trip participants and between participants and the environment, and two, it supplements the physical activities undertaken as part of the trip such as canoeing, hiking, or caving. To optimize the interpretation experience, it is necessary to develop an interpretative plan. This plan will identify:

· Information you want to convey

· Themes and sub-themes

· Characteristics of trip participants, such as age, culture, attitudes, interests, special needs, and expectations

· Methods of interpretation - demonstrations, living interpretations, signs, lectures, storytelling, and videos

· How interpretation activities will be evaluated

Keep in mind the full range of topics that can be included. While most include information on the natural setting, culture, and history, you should also consider land use and political issues. One of the ecotourism principles is to provide opportunities for people to become involved in local communities. By fully informing them about the challenges an environment is facing from human use, ecotourists can make choices about their actions. They may alter their buying habits after learning about the business practices of certain companies or they may make donations to non-profit groups providing school programs on environmental education.

Your interpretation plan should not be a static one. As conditions change or new opportunities arise, plan to bring these elements into your interpretation. If a group spots a rare bird or sees a comet, the guide should be able to work these events into the trip experience. Customer feedback should also be used to make changes to your interpretative plan. If people enjoy your discussions on specific plant species but would like more information on environmental or social issues in your area, add these to future trips.

QUALIFYING CUSTOMERS

If you are operating a tour company, one of the functions you should perform is qualification of customers. This is done for several reasons. One is safety. You want people to select trips that match their physical conditioning and comfort level. In this way they do not endanger themselves or the group and they enjoy the experience. Part of the qualifying procedure can also involve educating the client to the risks inherent in the activity they are undertaking. This may absolve the company of liability should an accident occur. An equally important reason for qualifying clients is to make sure people select a trip that matches their interests. This will enhance group dynamics and clients leave with memories of a great holiday.

It can be very difficult to qualify customers correctly. People can either over or under-estimate their physical condition. Their idea of a "nature experience" may not be yours. To avoid bad feelings, spend time learning about your prospective customers. In the competitive world of tourism marketing, the temptation is to book every person who calls. By understanding a little about the customer's interests and life-style, you can help them to choose the best trip. In some cases, that may be with your competitor!

It is also important to access a persons' physical ability to participate on a tour. Focus on identifying health conditions that may cause problems on the trip. Specific questions on physical conditioning, pre-existing medical conditions, special medications, and severe allergies will help match people to a particular tour or activity level. Questions should be standardized and asked of all prospective clients. While someone may look healthy, a bad back or a severe allergy to bee stings will require special preparation by your company to meet their needs. Questions you may want to use are:

- Do you understand the risk associated with (*activity*)?
- Is there any reason you may not be able to complete the tour?
- You understand that if you are unable to keep pace with the group, we would need to (*return to starting destination, radio for an airlift out of the backcountry, etc.*)?

Standardized questionnaires help avoid violating any legislation that prohibits discrimination against the elderly or disabled. On a more opportunistic note, if you find there are a number of prospective clients you are unable to accommodate for health reasons, you may be missing a marketing opportunity to provide an alternative experience.

To assess the interest level of prospective clients, one of the fastest ways is to ask questions about their previous vacations or recreational activities. Someone who is currently active in outdoor sports or who has taken camping or adventure trips in the past is likely to fit into an ecotourism experience. Those who have never been active

Qualifying customers may seem a difficult and tiresome task, but will pay for itself in the long run.

CASE STUDY: WHAT DO YOU DO ... WHEN THE WILDLIFE DOESN'T SHOW?

In the movie Jurassic Park, an irritating college professor asks the park owner, "Are there any dinosaurs on your dinosaur tour?" In real life, wise ecotourism operators know and prepare for the possibility that elusive wildlife will not show.

What do you do if your tour falls on the wildlife's day off? A well-planned tour with good content can be successful even without the wildlife. Calgary-based Mountain Quest proved this on a one-day trip to investigate wolves and their habitat in Banff National Park.

As seeing a wolf is not a common commodity, even for biologists studying them, it is important to schedule activities so trip participants still have a good time if the wolves aren't seen. As Trent Schumann of Mountain Quest said, "the trip is an interpretative tour of the area with the wolves as the subject as opposed to it being a wolf trip." It is a subtle difference but provides a worthwhile experience for the ecotourist. Led by Carolyn Callaghan, a wildlife biologist working on the Central Rockies Wolf Project, this trip included:

· A pre-trip seminar on wolf physiology, their behavior and habitat
· A visit to a field laboratory to see some of the scientific work underway
· The demonstration of radio tracking techniques. Trip members were able to try their hand at the tracking of the illusive 'test collar' hidden off the road.
· A visit to a viewpoint of the Banff valley and a visual explanation of the impact of development on wolf behavior
· Visits to a couple of kill sites, especially interesting for the action-orientated members of the group
· Tracking of wolf signals in the vehicle
· Following wolf and coyote tracks in the snow

All these ensured a full day for participants and ensured people came away with a better understanding of wildlife and the issues surrounding wolf survival.

And for icing on the cake - two wolves were spotted on this particular tour and spent the better part of an hour entertaining everyone with their movements and howling. An experience one never forgets!

Reprinted from: Kalahari Management Inc., *Ecotourism Management,* Spring 1996.

in outdoor recreation or who have traveled very little should not be ruled out; however, you have an obligation to spend more time explaining the tour components and the activity levels.

This requirement can be demonstrated by a real-life situation. An ecotourism company offering wildlife safaris in Africa had sold a luxury trip to a young woman who had spent little time outside of urban-settings. Even though it was billed as a tent-camp safari, the woman was dismayed to find out she was actually staying in a tent in the middle of the wilderness. Her discomfort affected the enjoyment of the entire group and she threatened to sue her travel agent for selling her that particular trip. Obviously, this is not the kind of word-of-mouth advertising you want. This could perhaps be avoided by spending more time qualifying clients.

KEY POINTS

- Customer service is an important way that ecotourism businesses can distinguish themselves from the competition.
- Every time ecotourists comes in contact with an organization, they will be judging the level of customer service.
- Delivery of customer service becomes more difficult as an operation grows. Proper procedures and training help ensure consistency of service.
- Interpretation is a unique feature of ecotourism operations. The ability to deliver interpretation is often underdeveloped by the ecotourism organization.
- Customers should be screened to ensure their physical and interest levels match those required for a trip.

WORKS CITED

1 Forestry Tasmania, *Guided Nature -Based Tourism In Tasmania's Forests: Trends, Constraints And Implications, Hobart*, Australia, 1994.

9 GETTING THE RIGHT PEOPLE FOR THE JOB

WHO DO YOU NEED?

Many ecotourism businesses are micro-businesses, a business with only one employee: the owner/manager. Others employ a handful of people and a few may have several hundred employees during peak seasons. Hiring staff is a challenge for many owners. The process can be uncomfortable, and if the wrong person is hired, it can be expensive to replace the employee and recover customers if customer-service problems occurred.

As an employer, you are responsible for employees' actions unless you can show otherwise. Given that many ecotourism employees lead groups into wilderness settings, the potential exists for physical harm and associated lawsuits if guides are not good at their job.

Staffing should be approached in a logical order.

Even the smallest operation will encounter staffing issues. You will probably delegate or hire out tasks to other people as you will not be able to do everything yourself. Many owners have strong knowledge of natural history, cultural resources, or are skilled at outdoor activities. While these skills are great, there are many other skills needed for success. Be honest. Are you good at selling? Bookkeeping? Tax planning? Designing internet advertising? To develop your business, it is essential to find the right people for these jobs.

Staffing should be approached in a logical order. That means identifying and grouping tasks together that require similar skills. A guide may not be a good typist, so you may need someone to handle correspondence and reservations. Take similar tasks and estimate the amount of time required to do each. This will give you an idea of whether you can add this work to someone already in the company or whether you need outside help, and whether the help should be full- or part-time, permanent or seasonal.

Write a job description similar to the example in Figure 9-1, outlining work to be done, performance standards, and level of supervision expected. Many small companies do not complete job descriptions, but a list of duties can clarify qualities and experience required of employees. This makes it easier to recruit and interview. It also helps ensure you are not discriminating against applicants, by having clear job duties and skill requirements.

131

A carefully prepared job description will help you weed out unsuitable employees in the hiring process.

Job descriptions point out holes in your organization, tasks no one gets around to, like prospecting corporate customers for incentive tours. "Holes" in your organization may be missed revenue opportunities. By identifying tasks that are not being completed, you can assess the value of adding, or not adding, a new employee.

Job descriptions also help identify employees whose skills do not match their job. Where you have a mismatch between employee and job, you may need to change their task set or hire another person who has a different skill set.

Detailed job descriptions help make hiring easier and guard against descrimination.

FIGURE 9-1 **JOB DESCRIPTION**

Title: River Guide

Job Description: To lead one day and overnight rafting trips

Job Duties:
- Provide input into trip planning and packaging
- Assess river conditions before trip launch and alter routes or launch points accordingly
- Ensure proper equipment available and in good repair
- Provide safety briefing to all trip participants
- Guide rafting trips incorporating historical and natural interpretation as conditions permit
- Coordinate meal times and camp set-up
- Educate trip participants on low impact travel techniques
- Monitor group dynamics and provide leadership, as required, to ensure the safety and enjoyment of all guests

Requirements:
- 3 years rafting experience
- Wilderness first aid
- Wilderness survival training
- Knowledge of natural history in area
- Cultural knowledge

Attributes:
- Strong interpersonal and leadership skills
- Ability to remain calm in times of crisis
- Responsible

HOW TO HIRE THE RIGHT PERSON

Finding qualified employees is difficult, especially in remote areas and in developing countries. If you are located close to a large urban center or popular recreation area, chances are there will be people who will meet your requirements. In other situations, you will find a limited pool of qualified employees, especially guides, in the local population. As one of the principles of ecotourism is to hire local people whenever possible to benefit the community, this poses a dilemma - Do you bring in experienced people to get your product to market quickly or do you develop guides and other personnel locally?

Do you bring in experienced people or develop guides and other personnel locally?

The solution is often unique to the situation. Some companies hire experienced outside guides to work with local people. This may provide opportunities for skills transfer between local staff and outside guides. An alternative is to train local guides. This is a longer-term solution but has the advantage of providing economic and social benefits to the community. You might reorganize jobs for flexibility in amount of work hours and scheduling so nontraditional labor is attracted. You can also structure your business so less labor is required. If you were planning a food service establishment as part of your business, it could be a cafeteria instead of a full-service restaurant.

Another special challenge is finding people with both interpretation and customer service skills. People in the industry have strong technical backgrounds but may be weak in interpretation. To provide a quality ecotour, they need to see through the eyes of the trip participants. If you are taking casual birdwatchers out for a bird watching tour, you will need to provide interpretation on the habitat and behaviors of birds. This will ensure a good trip even when a specie is not visible on the tour.

INTERVIEWING TECHNIQUES

Conducting a fair interview is important not only for legal reasons but also to make sure you hire the right person. Legal requirements vary from country to country. The next chapter explains the importance of hiring the right staff to avoid future lawsuits. Many books have been written on the hiring process. Those elements that merit special attention are:

- Use standard interview questions
- Include behavior interview questions to assess personal attributes
- Include a skills test
- Include a peer interview
- Avoid interview errors
- Do reference checks
- Verify qualifications

USE STANDARD INTERVIEW QUESTIONS - Standard interview questions establish a basis upon which to compare candidates' education, experience, skills, and training. Develop questions that will be used for all interviews. In addition, develop a range of acceptable answers and give each a numerical rating.

Being able to show the interviewing process was fair will help protect you from legal action.

By developing questions and answers in advance, subjectivity can be reduced considerably. Each candidate is asked the same questions and their answers are numerically scored. This avoids the common error of jumping to conclusions or hiring people because they are similar to the interviewer. It protects business owners legally as well, because the interviewing process can be demonstrated to be fair.

When developing your list of questions be sure to include probing queries that ask for specifics. Just because someone has been associated with a project or a special activity, do not assume the interviewee played a major role or has a particular skill.

Keep in mind employment and disabilities legislation precludes you from asking personal information that could be interpreted as discriminatory. The items that are often off-limits include age, marital status, ethnic background, religion, family, disabilities, sexual orientation, and criminal record. Instead of asking an interviewee whether they have a physical handicap, ask whether they can perform the requirements of the job. If you explain that the job requires them to hike five miles a day and they state that there is no reason why they cannot meet this requirement, you have some legal protection. If later they are unable to perform this task, you have grounds for dismissal, as they gave you assurance they were able to perform the job duties.

INCLUDE BEHAVIOR INTERVIEW QUESTIONS - To assess personal attributes including initiative and leadership, create questions based on past behavior. Behavior interview questions developed by Professor Tom Janz of the University of Calgary[1] are based upon the premise that the best predictor of future behavior is past behavior. If you want evidence that someone will deal well with customers, look for situations where they have demonstrated that skill in the past. This does not mean that someone has to have experience in exactly the same job; what you are looking for is some indication in a volunteer situation, other jobs, or school activities, that the candidate has worked well with customers.

Create questions based on past behavior.

A question you might ask is "Working as a hiking guide in remote situations can require you to resolve group conflicts without assistance from other people. Can you describe a situation where you resolved a conflict between customers in an isolated situation and what actions you took?" By asking for specific examples from their past, you have an idea of how that person will react in a specific situation. This is different from interviews where you ask a theoretical question: "Can you describe what actions you *would* take if you *were* faced with a conflict between customers in an isolated situation?" The answer may not reflect how someone has actually behaved. In addition, you can also standardize behavior interview questions by anticipating a range of acceptable answers and assigning corresponding numerical scores.

Use short, impromptu interpretative talks to assess a candidate's ability to think on his feet.

INCLUDE A SKILLS TEST - Given that ecotourists like to participate in a variety of activities and they value interpretation, you need guides who are skilled both in interpretation and outdoor pursuits. You can verify licenses and educational qualifications, but your best assessment of personal attributes, like interpersonal skills, comes from a well conducted interview. With a skill test, a candidate either has the skill or not. Giving people an unusual object from nature and asking them to give a short, impromptu interpretative talk will show a candidate's speaking skills and their ability to think on their feet.

INCLUDE PEER INTERVIEWS - If you have a small, closely knit team, it is important for new staff members to be accepted by everyone. Peer interviews can be incorporated by including a key staff member on the interview panel. Those people who score well on the initial interview could then be invited to an interview conducted by staff members. This interview can provide additional information on the candidates and ease their acceptance into the group. Peer interviews need to follow the same standards of interviewing mentioned earlier.

Think of your weaknesses and hire people who can compensate for them.

AVOID INTERVIEW ERRORS - If you have a small list of candidates, you may be tempted to select one who does not meet your basic requirements, rather than pursue additional candidates. You may also make a snap judgment about a candidate without going through a complete interview. You may place too much emphasis on nonverbal behavior; this can be a problem when hiring from cultures other than your own. For example, western culture values eye contact; other cultures may consider this disrespectful.

We are most comfortable with people like ourselves. This can translate into hiring someone who has your skills set and personality traits. If you are a very capable fishing guide, what you require may not be a person knowledgeable about fish but someone who knows how to sell your catch and release fishing trips. Think of your weaknesses and hire people who can compensate for them.

DO REFERENCE CHECKS - Take time to check the candidates' references. A few phone calls can confirm your impressions or smash them to bits. Ask questions that give you the information you want but do not violate employment and disability laws. Assess the person providing the reference. If they sound reserved or cautious in their praise, do not give extra weight to behavior.

You may find some companies do not provide references over the telephone. Legal

Where specific qualifications are a prerequisite, verify them.

action by employees who have received bad references without proper documentation has led companies to limit references to employee position and dates of employment.

VERIFY QUALIFICATIONS - Where specific qualifications are a prerequisite, verify them. Transcripts will confirm degrees or diplomas. Licenses or special training can be verified by contacting the licensing or delivery agency. Protecting your ecotourism business from legal risk requires you to hire people who are properly qualified. If an accident were to occur, you would not want to be found negligent because you had not taken reasonable steps to ensure your employees were licensed and trained for the job.

USING CONTRACT HELP

Higher payroll taxes and associated costs have made hiring employees an expensive process. Ecotourism businesses are most often seasonal or operating below capacity. Hiring full-time staff can be a financial commitment you cannot afford. An alternative is to engage a contractor who can deliver a service you need when you need it, for example - interpretation, sales, or catering.

Contracting services helps remove some administrative burden and frees the responsibility for payroll taxes. Some caution is required. The contractor must be a true business and not an employee presenting himself as a business. A problem arises when there is an employer/employee relationship but the employee is invoicing the company as a separate entity. Check employment and income tax legislation where you will be operating.

A contractor must be a true business, not an employee.

Another caution, you must ensure that contractors acting on your behalf meet your standards for customer service and safety management, as you could be liable for their actions.

TRAINING

In the previous chapter we talked about customer-service training. As part of your overall human resource planning, you should look at other areas where training is required. Where there is a gap between what you want employees to do and what they are capable of, you need to provide training. You can also consider adequate training as a safeguard to minimize liability (see Chapter 10).

When developing a training program, remember that training is the transfer of specific skills and behaviors; it is not the solution for all performance deficiencies. Before you put time and money into training, ask yourself if the employee can do the

---

FIGURE 9-1   IT PAYS TO KNOW ... IS THAT AN EMPLOYEE OR A CONTRACTOR?

With the boom in self-employment there are more and more people working in businesses who may not be actual employees.

While people may prefer to be treated as a contractor for tax reasons, the onus is on the employer to ensure that a employer/employee relationship does not exist.

In determining if a person is an employee, Revenue Canada will look for evidence of a "master/slave" relationship. This would be the ability to direct to a large extent the activities of the person doing the work.

Here are some specific "tests" that an employer should apply to a relationship to determine if they are hiring a contractor versus an employee.

A contractor generally:
· Has no fixed hours or work
· Is free to work for other companies while performing work for your company
· Hires his own assistants if required
· Controls day to day activities i.e. how work will be done/timing of activities
· Is employed for a specified time to complete a specified task
· Does not use company equipment or a company office

If an employer is found to have treated an employee as a contractor, the employer may be liable to pay all employee withholdings and the associated employer portions, including various penalties and interest payments. As fines can range in the thousands of dollars, it pays to review the employer/worker relationship carefully.

Reprinted from: Kalahari Management Inc., *Ecotourism Management*, Spring 1995.

---

task or will want to do the task. The first requires training, the second requires goal setting, feedback, and recognition. For businesses in remote communities or in developing countries, training requirements are generally higher. The areas where training is most often needed are:
· Natural history
· Culture
· Overview of ecotourism and its principles
· Code of ethics for guides and travelers
· Customer service
· Leadership and conflict resolution skills

· Equipment operation - boats, vehicles, radios, etc.

· Safety and survival tactics

· First aid

· Business skills such as marketing and business planning
(for owners and managers)

To develop a training program, consider the following steps:

ESTABLISH OBJECTIVES - What do you want employees to be able to do when training is complete? Be specific; do not say you want to develop great customer service. You need a measurable, observable activity. A training objective for an eco-lodge staff would be, "To learn to clean a room while adhering to sustainable tourism practices as set out in the company's environmental policy."

Objectives need to be specific and measurable.

SELECT DELIVERY METHODS FOR TRAINING - There are several methods of staff training that are useful to an ecotourism operator:

· On-the-job training

· Job-instruction training

· Training seminars

· Informal presentations or guest speakers at staff meetings

· Correspondence courses

· Training videos

On-the-job training is the most common and involves a knowledgeable employee teaching a new or inexperienced employee skills or behaviors. It is usually informal and costs are limited to the time required by both parties. Select people who have good training skills, not necessarily the most experienced. If you are training a new guide, assign training to a guide who provides interesting, enjoyable tours who can articulate how a successful trip is conducted. As people will also be transferring values and ethics, select employees who present your company in the best possible light.

For on-the-job training, select people who have good training skills and who will present your company in a positive light.

Job-instruction training is the use of a list of written sequential task descriptions. It works well for jobs that are task-orientated and could be helpful, for example, to a camp cook who may not be familiar with operating in an environmentally sensitive location. Job lists are relatively easy to prepare, provide consistent instruction, and do not require as much time from other employees to deliver training. The disadvantages are that you cannot ensure people use them, and in some cases, they may not understand the instructions.

Training seminars and workshops are a very visible form of training and provide concise, organized information on specific skills or behaviors. Training seminars will usually include a variety of techniques.

- Role playing
- Case studies
- Exercises
- Lectures
- Discussion
- Questioning

With few employees, it can be cost-effective to use external resources for training seminars. Tourism associations, chambers of commerce, industry associations, and universities all offer training appropriate for ecotourism. Larger organizations may chose to develop their own training. Training techniques should be selected for their suitability in transferring skills. For example, role playing is very helpful in training people in customer service, such as dealing with dissatisfied customers.

Ongoing training can be accomplished by informal presentations at regular staff meetings. These can be done by guest speakers or staff who have special skills. A local park ranger or historian can provide interesting insights on natural or historic points of interest.

Correspondence courses may be attractive where businesses operate in remote areas. Check with regional colleges and universities to determine which courses will be helpful.

Training videos can be especially helpful in smaller companies. Many business, education, tourism association, and special tourism education councils offer videos on topics relevant to your employees.

DELIVER THE TRAINING - The actual delivery of the training should be scheduled as close as possible to the employee's need for it. Shortly before the season starts would be a good time to provide customer-service training or train staff in low-impact camping techniques. The effectiveness of training is diminished when the skill is not used. Critical skills that are seldom used, such as first aid or search and rescue, need to be kept current through periodic practice sessions or drills.

EVALUATE TRAINING - At its very basic level, evaluation consists of asking people for their reactions to a training program. This will usually tell you if they enjoyed the experience. However, there may be no indication whether they actually learned from the program. A further method of evaluation is to test at the conclusion of training to see if they have learned the skills or behaviors. If so, you then can assess the extent to which the person transferred these skills to the job. Finally, ask yourself if the training brought the result you were seeking. For customer-service training, has feedback from customers been more positive? Have the number of repeat customers increased? For safety training, has the number or severity of accidents decreased?

HUMAN RESOURCE POLICIES

The mere mention of the word "policy" is enough to make some people run for cover. You may feel that your organization is too small to develop policies or that they will take away some of the flexibility and informal atmosphere that characterize your business. In fact, every owner or manager needs policies to ensure they treat people consistently and fairly.

A policy is a guiding principle for business operations on a particular topic.

A policy is a guiding principle for business operations on a particular topic. In addition to outlining how to handle situations regarding employee issues, policies can provide protection against lawsuits in employment and accident cases. For this reason alone, all businesses should have a policy manual and use it in daily operations. Areas where you need to think about your human-resource policies are:

- Sick leave
- Rates of pay
- Uniforms and dress codes
- Education, reimbursement or payment
- Hiring practices
- Termination procedures
- Benefits
- Work hours
- Safety

This is only a basic list; there are many other areas where you could develop policies. Policies do not have to be documented in great detail, but as your business grows, so will your need to develop and document your methods and principles.

MANAGING TURNOVER

Staff turnover is a cost that most businesses do not like to absorb. It is disruptive to business operations and adds expenses incurred in recruiting and training. Many people enter the industry for life-style reasons; however, they must still make enough money to support a base standard of living.

Small ecotourism businesses may not be able to provide full-time work. This could mean staff would be hired part-time by other businesses, reducing some of your scheduling flexibility or it could mean that staff will be hired away. Ways to minimize turnover are:

· Provide more earning opportunities
· Provide experience in a wider range of business activities
· Recognize employee efforts
· Use extra care in hiring to ensure a good job match
· Minimize conflict or the appearance of favoritism

Providing more earning opportunities requires finding business activities that give you additional income and your staff extra work hours. One way is to develop business activities which extend your operating cycle into the shoulder months. Add tours that focus on the fall foliage, visit cranberry festivals, observe fall or spring migrations, or examine ecological changes accompanying each season, such as a tour featuring a beaver lodge in winter.

A tourism company in northern Alberta - Ultimate Adventures - operates a water park for the community in addition to its main role as an ecotour provider. The operation of the water park provides a steady source of revenue for the company and stable work for some employees.

Many people realize that self-employment is the most likely route for a long-term career in the ecotourism industry. You can broaden employees' work opportunities by offering experience in marketing, trip planning or training, thereby offering more than financial compensation and increase their loyalty.

By offering employees special "perks," you cultivate company loyalty.

Another reason people become dissatisfied with the job is the lack of recognition from their employer. You may not be able to pay staff an exceptional good wage, however, you can "pay" them with a large amount of recognition. Catching people doing something right and showing your appreciation can go a long way in motivating people to go the extra mile and maintaining a stable work force. Ecotourism businesses are also blessed with the opportunity to offer in-kind products or services as a staff reward. Allowing employees to bring family or friends on a tour may not add much to your costs but can be a powerful reward. Some tourism companies swap product among themselves to reward employees for great customer service.

If you are still losing more people than you would like, consider your hiring practices. Are you hiring people who are inexperienced or have difficulty adjusting to remote locations or who find customer service difficult? Examine cases where you had good success with hiring. What type of qualifications or personal attributes did these people have that others did not? Perhaps you have employees who are overqualified for the job and they must leave to gain sufficient challenges. Conversely, you may be hiring people who are underqualified, and without training and coaching, become frustrated. Job descriptions

CASE STUDY: WHALE WATCHING IN BAJA MEXICO
by Brian Keating

In February of 1987 and again in February of 1996, I had the opportunity to experience a remarkable phenomenon in Baja, Mexico. I actually touched, repeatedly, wild grey whales, at what appeared to be their invitation.

Almost hunted to extinction by 1935, we now protect grey whales in their Pacific habitats. This has allowed the population to return to what some scientists believe to be almost prehunted levels, with numbers near 25,000 individuals. The grey whale has one of the longest migrations of any mammal, moving in the spring from the warm waters off the coast of Baja, Mexico up into the cold Alaskan waters where food is plentiful. They return again in the fall to breed and give birth in the Baja Lagoons.

The three major birthing lagoons along the 1,000 kilometer coastline of the peninsula are, from North to South, Scammon's Lagoon, San Ignacio Lagoon and Magdalena Bay. In these relatively quiet waters the grey whales come every winter to breed and give birth. Scammon's Lagoon, because of its size, is a difficult area for whale watching. It contains the most number of whales, but the individuals are more difficult to approach. Magdalena Bay is by far the most visited of the three lagoons. Because of its easily-reached geographic location, it receives many tourists, who have access to various modes of travel in the area. It is here the pressure of tourism has the potential to cause some difficulties, perhaps, with the biology of the whales themselves.

San Ignacio Lagoon is remote and difficult to approach by road and sea. It was here, twenty years ago, that a remarkable thing happened between a whale and some whale researchers. One day a grey whale came close, allowing the researcher to actually touch it! The researchers had many more similar encounters over the weeks to follow. Gradually, this behavior spread to other whales. Researchers have observed that female whales have been teaching this "friendly" behavior to their offspring, passing it down to successive generations. This has created a unique opportunity for whale watching enthusiasts. International maritime law dictates that oceanic vessels will not pursue whales, and in fact, are not to approach within a certain distance. However, when the whales decide to approach your boat it is an entirely different matter. The whale touching episodes are so consistent that ecotourism advertisements are now able to almost ensure this type of encounter.

In the early 1980s the Mexican government realized the importance of limiting access to San Ignacio Lagoon. Whales require space to "do their own thing," uninterrupted by the presence of tourists. As a result, only 20% of the lagoon itself was opened for tourists, and only one tourist boat within the lagoon is allowed to be anchored at any one point in time, with only three Zodiac boats each in the water. This highly controlled system persists today, although the government has eliminated the Zodiac boats. In their place, up to six pangas (Mexican fishing boats) may be used.

The Mexican government has recognized the importance of employing local fishermen during their winter season down time. Hence, this new tourism program idea has introduced a valuable, lucrative business for the local Mexican. I was incredibly impressed with their system, their integrity and obvious desire to do everything just right ... by the books. There was no indication of any kind of pursuit of the whales as we moved locations within the allotted area of the lagoon, and the guides' experience and patience enabled our group to experience numerous quality whale watching moments, including opportunities to touch. Having a forty-ton creature, often accompanied by a large baby, nuzzling up to the boat, inviting the hand of the tourist to touch, feel and massage the skin of the whale, is an exceptional experience.

The Mexican Government seems to be holding to its commitment of limited lagoon access, and the use of Mexican driven pangas as the sole means of whale encounters. Like the tourist program that enables individuals to visit the mountain gorillas of Central Africa, it appears the Mexicans are well on their way to developing an internationally renowned system of environmental tourism, following some of the classic examples already in place by some responsible governments and conservation organizations.

Brian Keating is Education Curator at the Calgary Zoo and is well known for his natural hsitory and travel commentaries on local and national media.

Reprinted from: *Ecotourism Management*, Kalahari Management Inc., Fall 1996.

---

can identify uneven matches between employee skills and job requirements. Where employees are known to be deficient, remedial training can be planned early in the employment period.

Tourism in North America is an industry characterized by high turnover; low wages and unusual work hours cause many to leave. Others enter the industry to gain experience or earn income to pursue other goals. This is changing slowly as people come to regard tourism jobs as viable careers. Ecotourism is not immune to these challenges; however, there are some differences. Ecotourism guides may be highly trained and have invested time and money to establish their credentials. This investment, accompanied with a passion for their sport or the outdoors, will provide employees who are motivated to find long-term, continuing employment. The emotional appeal of an ecotourism business, the marriage of conservation and business principles for mutual benefit, can also garner employee loyalty that may not exist in other tourism organizations.

KEY POINTS

· Ecotourism is foremost an experience in nature. Hiring the right guides and hospitality staff is critical in ensuring that the visitor experience is first-rate.

· Accreditation and certifications can be helpful in assessing technical skills. Rely on skill tests and interviews to assess interpersonal and leadership skills.

· Make sure legal obligations regarding employment are met. All steps of the recruiting and hiring process should be reviewed to ensure employment and disabilities legislation is complied with. Contract help should be assessed to determine if employee or contractor relationships exist.

· Human resource policies are helpful in maintaining staff morale and performance, and in avoiding employment legal action.

WORKS CITED

1 Tom Janz, Lowell Hellervik, and David C. Gilmore, *Behavior Description Interviewing,* Allyn and Bacon, Inc., Boston, 1986.

10

MANAGING BUSINESS RISK

IS ECOTOURISM DANGEROUS?

Ecotourism contains elements of nature, adventure, and cultural travel. It takes place in foreign lands and out-of-the-way places in your own country. Severe weather conditions, unexpected route changes, and encounters with animals bigger than you, are all potential parts of the experience.

This does not mean that ecotourism is dangerous; however, there is an element of risk in eco-travel. In fact, there is risk in all travel and in most activities we undertake, including the drive to the airport to start our eco-trip.

WHERE DOES RISK ORIGINATE?

People perceive the industry as being riskier than it actually is.

People perceive the industry as being riskier than it actually is. This can result in difficulties in obtaining insurance at affordable rates. The small but real threat of legal action requires a good understanding of where an ecotourism business is exposed to risk and actively working to minimize your exposure. Your ecotourism organization can face losses in the following areas.

PROPERTY DAMAGE - damage or loss to the physical assets of your business, such as a boat, building, or vehicle from theft, accident, fire, or vandalism.

BUSINESS INTERRUPTION - loss of earnings arising from a temporary stop in your business activity. If your operation was temporarily closed by fire, earnings would be interrupted and you might not be able to meet your financial obligations while you rebuild. Ecotourism businesses could also suffer losses if operating permits are cancelled or if severe or unusual weather conditions arise.

DISABILITY - Although many of us can claim good health today, there is a high possibility that we will be disabled at some point in our working lives. Most often the disability is short-term, a sprained ankle or pneumonia just before a trip, but in other cases, the disability is long-term or permanent. In both cases, employment income, and sometimes business income, is interrupted.

Loss of key individuals - Many companies rely on one or two special people in critical positions. It may be the owner of the company who is still the most popular guide for upper end clientele. The loss of key individuals could jeopardize the operation until a replacement is found.

Medical - If a customer were to be injured or become ill in a remote location, the evacuation or treatment of that person could become your responsibility.

Reduce your risk by implementing safety programs and contracting out some services.

Public liability - This is the area often associated with insurance claims and of particular interest to ecotourism providers. If someone is injured during a rafting trip or comes down with food poisoning on a day hike, you could be held responsible for the losses and stress suffered by that person, or in worst case scenarios, by that person's surviving family. You could also be held liable for the actions of contractors or suppliers you use to deliver part or all of your ecotourism product.

Losses in these areas could severely affect your business operations. To prevent this from occurring, you can take action in several areas. You can undertake a program of safety management to minimize the potential of accidents occurring in the first place. In conjunction with this, you can assess those areas where you have the greatest risk and obtain insurance to absorb the financial cost of an illness, accident, or property loss. You may also be able to reduce your risk by contracting out some services. If you contract with a canoe outfitter to provide canoes for your trips, the insurance for the canoes should be covered by the outfitter, resulting in lower insurance costs for you. Where you do use contractors, you need to clarify what risk they are assuming and obtain proof of insurance.

LEGAL LIABILITY

Of prime concern is the threat of legal action arising from the operation of your business. The areas most relevant to ecotourism providers are:
- Tort claims
- Doctrine of respondeat superior
- Contract law
- Product liability

TORT CLAIMS - include liability for negligence or gross negligence. If an operator is found to have not acted carefully in a circumstance (negligence), or even when facing danger acted with some degree of recklessness (gross negligence), he may be liable to the customer. While the use of waivers may prevent losses in the case of negligence, they may not be effective where gross negligence is proven. Another possible tort claim can arise in the area of strict liability. If an activity is found to be "inherently dangerous" by a jury, the operator could be liable.

DOCTRINE OF RESPONDEAT SUPERIOR - An employer is responsible for the actions of employees as they execute their job duties. It extends responsibility for negligence from the individual employee to the employer.

CONTRACT LAW - Involves the many agreements signed between operators and their suppliers and clients. Suppliers who fail to deliver services as set out in the agreement would be liable under contract law for losses incurred. If you advertise specific experiences or accommodation quality, you could be held liable if you do not deliver as advertised.

PRODUCT LIABILITY - A concern for operators who provide equipment for their tours. If a product fails and injury results, the customer could take legal action. For this reason, it best to deal with equipment manufacturers who sell high-quality equipment and stand behind their product, i.e. they carry insurance for this situation.

INSURING AGAINST THE ODDS

To mitigate the consequences of legal action or to soften the loss of property or income, insurance is desirable. In some cases, it may be mandatory. Before you are able to obtain licenses or permits in many national parks, you are required to have proof of public-liability insurance.

Justified or not, many insurance companies perceive ecotourism and adventure travel as high risk and charge higher premiums, or in many cases, choose not to offer insurance at all. Make sure insurance cost is factored into the cost of your product. Where a trip requires higher insurance premiums, there should be a higher price.

Finding a good carrier may take some work. Ask other ecotourism operators in your area what insurance companies they use and make inquiries through them. Compare rates to ensure you are receiving the best rate. Be prepared to spend several hundred dollars annually on public-liability insurance for "low risk" activities such as guided nature hikes. White-water rafting, kayaking, or roped climbing may cost thousands of dollars, if you are even able to obtain insurance.

Location also influences insurance costs. If you are leading trips in North America, your public-liability insurance premiums will be higher than in developing countries, where you might not be able to obtain insurance. You may instead rely upon a local operator to provide insurance coverage.

Unfortunately, some operators are unable to obtain insurance for an activity or cannot afford the premiums. They may elect to operate in areas where insurance is not required and hope that no accidents occur. Often they have few assets or have structured their company so their personal liability is minimized. This harms the industry as a whole, as consumers are not properly protected. Operators playing by the rules are at a disadvantage when pricing their product against someone who is not carrying the same level of insurance.

If your assets are small, you may decide to self-insure.

TYPES OF INSURANCE - Insurance coverage corresponds to the types of losses discussed earlier, specifically:
- Property damage
- Public liability
- Business interruption
- Disability
- Loss of key individuals
- Medical

In each situation, evaluate the likelihood of loss, the impact of such a loss on your business, and whether you are legally required to carry insurance. You may be required to carry public liability insurance but may feel that property damage is something you need not insure. If your assets are small and you could replace the equipment and carry on in the event of accidental loss, fire or vandalism, you may decide to use savings to self-insure. Use Figure 10-1 below to plan your insurance requirements.

SAFETY MANAGEMENT - MINIMIZING YOUR RISK

Ensuring the safety of your customers is one of the most important functions you will undertake. While you can insure yourself for lawsuits arising from accidents, there is no insurance that will cover your financial cost from lost customer goodwill.

Ecotourists in some cases are looking for an element of adventure in their trips. Most expect they will enjoy their experience without being placed in peril. If cus-

FIGURE 10-1 INSURANCE REQUIREMENTS

Category	Insurance Coverage Required ($)	Estimated Annual Cost ($) Carrier	Possible Insured	Loss if not
Property damage	50,000	350.00		
Public liability	2,000,000	2,000.00		
Bus. interruption	200,000	200.00		
Disability	50,000	1,000.00		
Loss of key individuals				
Medical				
Total Cost	$	$3,750.00	$	$

tomers are placed in dangerous situations, damage to your reputation may take considerable time to overcome.

The secret to successful safety management is to provide an element of perceived risk without significant actual risk to the customer. Climbing schools have been managing this balance for years. They know that by "top roping" clients, they provide the thrill of scaling rock faces or walls, without any real danger of the climber falling. Ecotourist operators need to apply the same safety management principles. People should feel adventure in their experience but it should be from situations where there is no danger.

Ensuring the safety of your customers is one of the most important functions you will undertake.

ACCIDENT POTENTIAL - It is helpful to look at a model of accident potential. The model shown in Table 10-1 was developed by Rick Curtis of the Outdoor Action Program at Princeton University. It shows accident potential is based upon a number of factors.

Where there are more "hazards" present, the probability of an accident is greater. In fact, where environmental hazards and human factor hazards are combined, the effects are multiplied, not added. If there are two Environmental Hazards and two Human Factor Hazards there is a four times higher accident potential. If there are three Environmental Hazards and three Human Factor Hazards there is a nine times higher accident potential[1]. With the potential for accidents increasing at this rapid rate, it makes sense to minimize hazards through sound planning and daily management.

A solution is to look at environmental factors. While you cannot control the weather, you can control your reaction to it. Establish procedures that require guides to obtain a weather forecast before setting out, or insist that guides and participants carry clothing that is waterproof or good for snow. Set policies that stipulate no trips will be taken if temperatures drop below a certain level. In the event that rain, mud, or snow makes

---

TABLE 10-1 DYNAMICS OF ACCIDENTS MODEL

Environmental Hazards	x	Human Factor Hazards	=	Accident Potential
· Terrain · Weather · Equipment		· Physical condition · Experience · Skills · Fear · Communication		*To determine risk of accident potential add up the number of negative environmental or human factors. Where environmental and human factors are combined, the effect is multiplied, not added.*

Source: Rick Curtis, *Outdoor Action Program*, Princeton University, 1995.

a route impassable, develop alternate routes. Have practice events, announced and unannounced, to test your contingency plans in the event a group is overdue.

The other side of the equation is people. In this area you can normally exert some form of direct control to minimize accident potential. Help your guides be prepared and properly qualified, and do the same with your customers.

While guides may need to be certified, especially for adventure sports, there are often no certifications required for hiking, birdwatching, or nature observation. Whether it is an adventure trip or a butterfly hike, there is a need for all guides to have certain basic skills to minimize risk. These include the ability to recognize risk and find acceptable solutions.

As a minimum, you want guides to be trained in wilderness first aid, survival, map reading, group control, communication skills, and radio operation. Certification gives you an indication of a person's skill in a particular activity, but it is not an indication of their ability to lead a group safely.

You do not want to find yourself in a crisis situation where your most experienced canoe guide paddles down river first, leaving minimum instructions, or setting routes that are too long for the ability and stamina of the group. These increase potential of accidents.

QUALIFYING CLIENTS - The people taking your ecotourism experience should also be qualified. This can be done by a short questionnaire or by talking to each in person. Determine whether people are in the physical condition needed to safely enjoy your trip, and whether their personality and personal preferences are such that they will have a good time. There is no sure way of knowing this in advance. Asking people to complete a standardized questionnaire and inquiring about their past trips or outdoor hobbies can determine how they spend their time, what types of activities they enjoy, and capabilities. Asking for a doctor's certificate of sound health may also be appropriate in some cases, but check regional and federal legislation to ensure such requests are legal.

STEPS TO A SAFER TRIP - When you break down accident potential into the components of environmental and human factors, there are many actions you can take to make trips as safe as possible (see Figure 10-2).

Incorporate proper hiring, training, safety, customer qualifications, and other similar principals into your company's operation. You will significantly reduce the potential for accidents and losing a lawsuit. More importantly, you reduce the possibility of losing your good name.

To date, ecotourism businesses have not had significant numbers of accidents or injuries. This demonstrates that skill and planning can go a long way in reducing accident potential. Ecotourism operators need to maintain this diligence to ensure accident rates remain low. It is a temptation to continue an early season trip in bad weather when cashflow is low. However these short-term revenue gains may seriously jeopardize future revenue.

IF THE WORST HAPPENS - Even with good planning, policies, and training, accidents can happen. If so, it is important to react correctly. Document events and existing conditions; use a standardized form to gather pertinent accident information. It is easy to forget important details. Contact your insurance company and the proper authorities in a timely manner. A contact person for media inquiries should be determined so a consistent message is presented. Concern for the person who is injured or suffered a loss is a priority. While you do not want to admit liability, companies often exacerbate the situation by giving the impression they do not care what has befallen their client.

ASSET PROTECTION

In addition to securing insurance and continually improving your safety management program, you can also protect your company by the way it is legally structured. A sole proprietorship exposes both the owner and the business to legal action. Personal assets could be lost in a successful lawsuit. Incorporating your business to form a Limited Company can remove some of this risk by limiting liability in most cases to the assets of the company. Some take this a step further and create several companies. One that offers activities with risk would hold few assets. Another company, the parent or holding

FIGURE 10-2   STEPS FOR A SAFE ECOTOURISM OPERATION

Some things you can incorporate into the safety management program of your ecotourism company are:

· **Planning** - Select alternate trip routes and activities that can be used in inclement weather or if the energy level of the group is waning.

· **Policies** - Set policies on how many guides will accompany a trip. (In some sports and states, minimum guide numbers may be already set by governing agencies.) Develop safety policies that provide direction for bad weather, approaching wildlife, communicating with the base location, and other items that are relevant to your operation.

· **Hiring** - Look for personal attributes like judgment, leadership, and communication skills, as well as appropriate certification when hiring guides. Check references from previous employers to assess the guide's performance under difficult conditions.

· **Training** - Provide training in leadership skills so that guides can maintain control over a group under stress. If bad weather is encountered and disagreements arise over the best way to continue the trip, your guide must be able to prevent part of a group from trying to find their own way back to the trail head.

· **Qualifying clients** - Ensure that all clients have completed a questionnaire and in cases where physical condition is critical or a person has had medical problems, insist on a doctor's examination before the trip departs. Match the customers abilities and interests to activities and tour itineraries. Help the customer select a tour that is a good choice for them. Resist the temptation to add them to a trip that is beyond their capabilities because you need the extra people in order to run the trip.

· **Equipment** - Mechanical failure from equipment can significantly increase the potential of accidents. Make it a priority to examine all equipment and restore it to good working order. Where equipment is nearing the end of its life, budget funds to replace it.

· **Practice** - Give your staff the chance to practice their safety skills, especially those that are used only in times of crisis, such as first aid or rescue drills.

· **Waivers** - Prepare waivers for customers to sign advising them of the risks of the activity they are about to undertake and absolve you of responsibility in the event of an accident, injury or illness. While waivers may not prevent lawsuits, they can reduce the likelihood that someone would win a claim against your business as you will have made them aware of the potential risks and dangers beforehand.

company of the first, is where the majority of assets would reside. While this may not offer complete protection in a legal action, it can provide added safety for a business owner.

KEY POINTS

- Ecotourism can present risk because of the nature of activities and that much time is spent outdoors, often in remote locations.
- Risk originates both from the environment and from the people involved in the ecotourism activity.
- Environmental risk can be addressed through safety management. This could include planning alternate routes, setting criteria against which go/no-go decisions are made, and ensuring equipment is replaced before the end of its useful life.
- Minimizing risk from people requires proper hiring and training of staff and careful screening of customers.
- Some types of insurance, such as public-liability insurance, may be required by law. In other cases, it is prudent to purchase insurance to compensate for financial losses when situations go awry, such as fire or employee illness.
- Managers should be aware of what risks they are responsible for. A travel agent or tour packager can be held responsible for the actions of a supplier. Developing careful criteria for selecting suppliers, documenting transactions, and obtaining proof of insurance can mitigate exposure.

WORKS CITED

1 Curtis, Rick, *Outdoor Action Program*, Princeton University, 1995.

11   BUSINESS PLANNING

THE NEED FOR A BUSINESS PLAN

Ecotourism businesses often operate with small margins and must make enough money in the peak season, often only a few months long, to maintain the business from year to year. The competition for the consumer's disposable income and free time is not just with other providers but also with shopping centers, video rentals, and golf courses. Add to this the government legislation that must be understood and complied with, and you have a business that requires detailed planning and careful management.

As you work through the development of product, marketing, and financing, you will appreciate the need for a business plan. It is your blueprint for the next several years. By writing a business plan, you will utilize resources better, minimize problems, prepare for the unexpected, and have a better chance of success.

A business plan will not prevent all problems but can head off many by making you aware of areas where you are vulnerable. For example, if your business plan identifies a cashflow problem at the start of your operating season, you can plan ahead by obtaining a line of credit instead of having angry creditors and harming your credit rating.

ELEMENTS OF A BUSINESS PLAN

Your business plan will have elements similar to those of other businesses, including:

- Executive summary
- Description of products or services
- Marketing plans: the ecotourism market and your targeted customers, an analysis of your competitors, marketing strategies, and sales forecasts
- Management: key personnel and legal structure of company

· Operations: location, environmental considerations, equipment requirements

· Financial forecasts: projected income statement, projected balance sheet, projected start-up costs, and financing requirements

· Appendices

YOUR AUDIENCE

When writing your business plan, keep in mind your reasons for preparing it.

Business plans are prepared for a number of reasons:

· To communicate business concepts, marketing strategies, and financial forecasts

· To obtain external financing

· To clarify your strategies, challenges, and operating activities

· To communicate your ecotourism goals and strategies within your organization

When writing your business plan, keep in mind your reasons for preparing it. If you are hoping to attract investors, remember that the plan is also a marketing tool. You must excite the reader about your business. Show them you have done your research. While you do not want to stretch the truth, use a colorful style of writing that conveys the special sense of your product. In ecotourism, you are often selling the experience. Describing the intangibles by which people will remember your trip requires a bit of effort but is necessary to communicate those attributes that make your business special.

THE ECOTOURISM DIFFERENCE

Your commitment to the environment should be reflected in your mission statement.

Your business plan will differ from other businesses plans because of your commitment to the environment and responsible operating practices. This commitment should be reflected in the mission statement and in each part of product development and delivery.

· Are you selling kayaking tours or are you selling lifetime memories of a natural history experience? The subtle ways in which you look at your product can have a big difference in how you promote your product and how you distinguish your tour or service from a non-ecotourism product when marketing.

· Your environmental commitment requires additional consideration in the operations section to minimize visitors' impacts.

· There may be permits or special equipment required for sensitive areas.

· You may discuss the development of policies to ensure staff operate in an environmentally responsible way.

- You may discuss alliances with non-profit organizations or community groups to help you meet the goal of supporting conservation activities and local communities.
- Your Operations section may detail how you plan to use local suppliers.
- Financial forecast may present special challenges. Many ecotourism businesses are seasonal in nature and due to the environmental sensitivities of remote areas, may have small group sizes. This can result in low revenues and higher start-up costs, which obviously leads to reduced profits. This may require some creativity in developing ways to repay investors.

Before preparing your plan, brainstorm on these differences and the unusual features of your area. A list of unique problems and opportunities will help you to write a better plan as you build management strategies to deal with each.

PREPARING THE PLAN

When developing your business plan, include information on each major business area. Detailed information on marketing, financing, human resources, and operations is found throughout this book and can be referred to as the plan is developed.

The legal structure and background on key management personnel is of added importance if you are presenting your business plan to external parties. Each section is described briefly in the following sections.

An executive summary gives readers a powerful introduction to your business.

EXECUTIVE SUMMARY - This section is a short synopsis (one to two pages) of your business, highlighting your business concept, marketing plans, forecasted financial requirements/results, and operations. By condensing the key elements of your business plan into a few pages, the executive summary gives readers a powerful introduction to your business and the unique features that distinguish it.

For companies using the business plan to secure outside financing or investment, it is critical that the executive summary be well written. It should be a concise, thoughtful outline, written in a manner to catch the reader's attention. Investors are often faced with scores of business plans, your plan must capture their interest quickly.

DESCRIPTION OF PRODUCTS OR SERVICES - This section describes the products or services you will provide. This may sound so obvious that it does not bear mentioning; however, many people are at a loss to explain their business concept clearly and succinctly. You should be able to describe your business in a few sentences. If it takes you several pages to describe the concept, chances are the product will require lengthy explanation to sell it to customers, or it may not sell at all.

Without evidence that a market exists for your business, your dreams may be over before you get started.

MARKETING - The marketing section includes the most important information from your marketing plan. Your situation analysis, market analysis, and competitive analysis will be used to explain why your product is marketable and to estimate market size. The marketing description will provide details on target market segments, pricing of your product, advertising strategies, potential market share or sales volumes, and information on competitors.

This section will explain the overall characteristics and size of the ecotourism industry, then focus on the ecotourism market in your area and on the portion of the market you think you will capture. Investors or lenders may not be familiar with ecotourism, so you need to include a brief description of other ecotourism operators in your area and their strengths and weaknesses. This competitive analysis will show how you will compete against other ecotourism or recreation organizations. Without that distinction, and evidence that a market exists for that uniqueness, your ecotourism dreams may be over before you get started.

While the financial forecasts (explained in Chapter 7) may be the first thing that people look at in your business plan, a savvy investor knows that the accuracy of those numbers depends upon the marketing plan. The forecasted sales volumes come from the marketing plan and are the starting point for financial forecasts; therefore, sales forecasts are very important when assessing the viability of your business.

MANAGEMENT - This section discusses the structure of your business and includes key personnel backgrounds. Having management personnel with industry/management experience is a predictor of success. Investors look carefully at key people for experience in related businesses. Unfortunately, tourism or recreational business experience may not carry much credibility with banks, and owners may have to provide personal guarantees. No matter, it is essential to describe management. What are your strengths? Where are your gaps in knowledge or experience? If you are not good at marketing or do not know a debit from a credit, you may need other people to help run your business. Evaluating management structure identifies where you need to bring in other people.

Having management personnel with industry or management experience is a predictor of success.

The sections also include a description of your business legal structure: sole proprietorship, partnership, or an incorporated entity. Each has its own advantages and disadvantages (Table 11-1). For a community-based venture, a non-profit organization may be created. Consider which structure meets your needs. Many ecotourism ventures are small businesses and seasonal in operation. A sole proprietorship offers ease of start-up and lower costs; however, an incorporated entity or limited company will provide more protection in the event of legal action.

OPERATIONS - This section describes all the physical characteristics of your business.

TABLE 11-1 **LEGAL STRUCTURES**			
	Sole Proprietorship	**Partnership**	**Limited Company**
Advantages	Easy to start up Fewer costs associated with maintenance e.g. annual returns	More growth opportunities than a proprietorship Investment by two or more people	Liability limited for third parties Existence not limited to shareholders' lives Can have one or more owners
Disadvantages	One owner Unlimited owner's liability Limited to owner's life Personal income tax rates apply to withdrawals of profits	Limited to partner's lives Liable for partner's actions Personal tax rates apply on withdrawal of profits	Company profits taxed at corporate rates Investment possible in several forms Incorporation costs incurred to establish, other costs required to maintain

For an ecotourism business, that may not be the actual office location but, rather, the protected area where the trips occur. Ecotourism's emphasis on the environment presents unique operational challenges as follows.

- How will you operate your business: equipment, staff, human-resource strategies, management style, insurance requirements?
- How will your business address different activities or profit centers, such as gift shops or bed & breakfast inns?
- How will you obtain required permits/licenses that you do not hold, and what will be the impact on your business if you cannot obtain them or the cost is greater than expected? By identifying where you hold or reasonably expect to obtain licenses, you provide support for sales forecasts.
- How will an environmental impact assessment rate your business?
- What is the impact of your business on the physical and cultural environments? Key indicators and the methods to measure indicators should be identified as time progresses.
- Will you make donations of cash or in kind to conservation groups? Will you share information on animal observations with park managers or wildlife scientists?
- What will be the special care you take with waste management, especially in remote locations?
- How will you handle transportation systems to move building or operating supplies - people with backpacks or wheelbarrows, pack animals, or helicopter drops?

FINANCIAL FORECASTS - This section outlines the cost of starting or improving your business and the operating revenues and expenses that you expect over the next year or more. You should include a *proforma* (forecasted) balance sheet and cash flow projections, as well as a break-even analysis. You may include your personal assets/liabilities and net worth if financing is sought. You may also include a summary of start-up costs/ capital improvements and the proposed financing. The schedules that will be included in the financial section of the business plan are: *proforma* (forecasted) income statement, cash flow forecasts, *proforma* (opening) balance sheet, schedule of start up costs, summary of financing requirements and sources, and statement of net worth. Detailed information on these schedules is found in Chapter 7 and in the Business Plan Workbook accompanying this book.

*When completing start-up cost schedule, be sure to include **all** possible costs.*

When completing your start-up cost schedule, be sure to include all possible costs.
· Equipment
· Land or buildings
· Vehicles
· Advertising campaigns
· Inventory (food, spare parts, clothing, promotional material, etc.)
· Licenses, permits
· Environmental impact assessment
· Operating costs until break-even is reached (rent, electricity, payroll, insurance)
· Contingency amount
· Draws and salaries

A worksheet for start-up costs is shown in Section 6-3 of the workbook. The schedule in Figure 11-1 summarizing financial requirements and sources may be helpful in presenting your financing requirements to lenders or investors. It shows where you have invested capital and secured other investors. Possible financing sources are:
· Trade credit
· Mortgage loan
· Leasing
· Commercial loan
· Government subsidy
· Line of credit
· Owner's investment
· Equity investment or loans by private investors

Figure 11-2 FINANCIAL REQUIREMENTS AND PROPOSED FINANCING SOURCES	
FINANCIAL REQUIREMENTS	
Licenses and permits	$ 5,000
Marketing campaign	10,000
Computer	5,000
Operating costs until break even	30,000
Total Financial Requirements	**$50,000**
PROPOSED FINANCING	
Bank loan	$ 5,000
Line of credit	10,000
Government subsidy	3,000
Trade credit	2,000
Owner investment	30,000
Total Financing	**$50,000**

Use this helpful schedule when presenting your financing requirements to lenders or investors.

Once you have completed the financial forecasts, you would be wise to conduct a break-even analysis or a sensitivity analysis. A break-even analysis tells the level of sales needed to meet your operating costs and start generating a profit. If forecasted sales are below your break-even point, you need cash on hand or financing until you reach your break-even point.

A sensitivity analysis tries to answer "what if?" Ecotourism is a new industry; your sales projections could be wrong by 10 percent, 20 percent, or more. As you gain experience and as the marketplace grows, these projections will improve. A sensitivity analysis shows what will happen to profits if your sales volume is 10 percent less than forecasted, or if you sold more of one type of tour than planned. (Break-even and sensitivity analyses are discussed in Chapter 7.)

APPENDICES - There will always be information that won't fit neatly into the body of your plan and should be included in the business plan as an appendix. These materials may be lengthy or voluminous such as:

- Permits
- Contracts
- Licenses
- Purchase contracts
- Marketing agreements
- Maps
- Brochures
- Prior financial statements

- Key personnel resumes
- Letters of support from community organizations
- Environmental impact assessment studies
- Primary market research
- Surveyor certificates
- Proof of insurance coverage
- Background on community partners
- Competitor analysis details

BUSINESS PLAN WORKBOOK

Allowing enough time to write a detailed business plan is time well spent.

Included with *The Business of Ecotourism* is an Appendix that contains a workbook to assist you in completing your business plan. It is a guide for gathering business plan information. Once each area has been researched, you will have a much better idea of the direction your business will need to take and the challenges and opportunities you will face along the way.

Again, the presentation (format and style) is important if you are showing it to lenders, investors, or staff. If you are the primary user, you can keep the written descriptions brief or summarize information in point form as you will have all the detailed information on hand.

Allow enough time to write the business plan. It may take weeks or months, but it is time well spent. The enclosed workbook provided by *The Business of Ecotourism* will reduce the effort required to summarize data and prepare financial forecasts. There are a number of business plan software packages on the market. However, it is unlikely you will find one tailored to your operations. You can start with a basic template and modify it to meet your specific needs. Many banks provide business-planning software at a nominal charge.

KEY POINTS

- A business plan is a solid blueprint for the marketing, operations, and financial management of a business.
- Know the target audience. Length of time spent on the business plan and level of detail depend on its ultimate use.
- A business plan is critical when securing financing.
- Ecotourism businesses are similar to other businesses, but there are unique features: the market, the care taken to minimize environmental impacts, and the remote and seasonal nature of operations. These should be highlighted.
- A business plan prepared only for owner use does not require as much explanation as a plan that will be presented to other audiences.

12   INDUSTRY STANDARDS
AND ASSOCIATIONS

INDUSTRY STANDARDS: NEEDED OR NOT?

Whenever you have a business, tourism or otherwise, operating in natural settings, the potential for harm exists. While some ecotourism advocates have argued for no-impact travel, most agree that all travel has some impact; what we are striving for is to minimize impact and compensate for the impact by contributing positively to the economy and social fabric of the communities visited.

The need for standards arises out of the difficulty to determine an organization's philosophy and commitment to sustainable tourism.

What makes ecotourism unique is the philosophy behind it - the desire to see tourism developed and operated sustainably so future generations may enjoy the same places we do. People argue that ultimately all tourism must be operated sustainably for us to survive, and therefore all tourism becomes ecotourism. However, at this point, there are vast differences in the environmental programs adopted by tourism providers. Because it is difficult to determine an organization's philosophy and commitment to practices of sustainable tourism, the need for standards arise.

Industry standards are increasingly recognized as mechanisms to ensure the integrity of the tourism product, as well as increase marketability and credibility with the traveling public.

THE ROLE OF ECOTOURISM STANDARDS

Standards clarify what is required for a tour or hotel operator, transportation provider, attraction, or other tourism organization to be considered "environmentally responsible" and "sustainable."

While many tourism organizations support and claim to operate in an environmentally sustainable manner, the definition of standards ensures a common agreement on sustainable tourism practices. Standards could accomplish the following:
· Define sustainable tourism practices clearly
· Provide external validation of adherence to sustainable tourism practices
· Measure compliance against established criteria

163

Standards establish measurable criteria for tourism development and operation.

· Provide consistency in the use of sustainable-tourism labels or claims
· Reduce confusion among travelers looking for ecotourism products
· Increase marketability of providers meeting the criteria

We often turn to the principles of ecotourism to assess whether an organization is an ecotourism venture. Standards would refine that process further by establishing measurable criteria for tourism development and operation.

Identifying the ecotourism product for tourists is another benefit of standards. A certification process, whereby organizations are recognized for meeting responsible-tourism standards would provide quality control to the traveler and make the selection of products and services easier.

The question of whether a certification process would increase the marketability of a nature or culture-based company has not yet been proven. At the time of writing there are several ecotourism standard and certification programs in place. Many people recognize the need for more research in this area.

MAINTAINING STANDARDS INTEGRITY

To establish industry-wide standards is a very large undertaking. Industry stakeholders need to reach consensus on the definition of sustainable tourism practices. With the diverse range of business types, each one may require distinct standards, making the process more complex and prone to conflict.

Compliance with standards can be an important aspect of a marketing program.

Standards do exist in the form of voluntary guidelines. The International Ecotourism Society has published a set of guidelines that are environmentally-friendly, community-based practices for ecotourism operators. The problem with voluntary guidelines is the extent to which compliance is left to the individual organization. While no formal recognition is given for the adoption of these standards, compliance with them can be an important aspect of a marketing program and should not be ignored.

Along with the standards comes the certification process to rate an organization's compliance with adopted standards. An organization receives certification when it meets the minimum standards. Implementing an industry certification process requires money to develop and maintain the standards, certify organizations, and inform businesses and the traveling public about certification. A logical source of funding would be those who would benefit from the process. Tourism operators are able to market their adherence to sustainable tourism standards and could use this to justify the certification cost. A conflict of interest arises where those receiving certification are those providing the funding. Organizations not receiving certification may withdraw their financial support.

An alternative would be the creation of an independent government organization able to grant certification. This approach is unlikely due to shrinking government budgets.

Perhaps the best hope for the future comes from the traveling public. If tourists demand a high level of environmental responsibility from tourism providers, the additional sales to be made by being a "green" tourism operator would provide financial incentive to adopt and promote environmental standards.

EXISTING PROGRAMS

There are programs emerging to identify responsible tourism providers. The largest of these are described below. Most represent a commitment to responsible tourism practices, not evidence of actual sustainable practices. Little monitoring occurs and there are few formal enforcement procedures. As these processes grow, there will be a need to correct compliance problems to preserve the integrity of the accreditation process.

GREEN GLOBE - This program was developed by the World Travel and Tourism Council and is open to companies of any size, type, or location. Green Globe is a non-profit entity whose goals are to:
  · Provide a means for companies to commit to environmentally-friendly business practices
  · Distribute information on the best environmental management practices
  · Allow companies to display their commitment through the Green Globe logo

To qualify, members complete a benchmark process on their business practices regarding the environment and host communities. They then undertake a certification process. Members are encouraged to use the Green Globe logo to demonstrate their adherance to standards.

The program is financed through annual membership fees based upon annual gross receipts, and can vary from a few hundred to a few thousand dollars. Contact: *Green Globe, customer.services@greenglobe.org.*

GREEN LEAF - This program is sponsored by Audubon International for the hospitality industry and is open to members of any size. The objectives are to:
  · Help hotels assess and improve their environmental capabilities.
  · Show hotels how being eco-efficient reduces costs and increases market share.
  · Allow companies to display their environmental commitment with the Green Leaf logo
  Organizations apply for accreditation by completing a self-assessment questionnaire on general tourism practices and sector-specific practices. It is then scored by Terra

Choice Environmental Marketing. Companies recieve a rating and a technical report that will allow them to improve their environmental performance.

One fee covers the survey, marketing manual, a list of recommendations, written technical report, a visit from a rating auditor and a posting on the Web. For more information, contact Audubon Green Leaf Eco-Rating Program at www.terrachoice.com.

Eco Certification - This is a unique certification program developed for tourism operators in Australia but often touted as a possible model for certification programs worldwide. The program certifies products, not companies, and provides two categories of certification: nature tourism and ecotourism. Ecotourism certification has two levels, each of which has more stringent requirements.

Companies complete a detailed application that is then forwarded to an independent Assessor. This person reviews and scores the application and contact independent referees for confirmation of information presented. Members pay a three year membership fee as well as an application fee. For more information, contact Ecotourism Australia at www.ecotourism.org.au.

INDUSTRY ASSOCIATIONS

Industry associations are a valuable way to strengthen nature and culture-based tourism operators and can provide a collective vision on environmentally friendly tourism, responsible standards or guidelines, a collective voice to influence government policies, a way to share information, greater presence and marketability, an ability to share marketing costs.

Some regions are leading the way with these efforts. The Texas Nature Tourism Council focuses on information sharing and marketing Texas nature-tourism products. South Carolina has formed a nature-tourism association to share information and promote visitation. Other regions are developing similar associations as the industry grows and the benefits of such associations are seen.

Industry associations are valuable tools for ecotourism operators.

Steps To Establishing An Association - Developing a nature-based association requires community support and a well-defined set of objectives, along with much hard work. The following steps should be incorporated.

• Obtain community support. Listen to community representatives to determine their concerns. Find out what they want the future to look like, for the community or the organization. Talk to people from all walks of life, such as business leaders, environmental groups, government agencies, elected officials, school representatives, service groups, retired people, families, etc. People not directly involved in tourism will be affected by tourism and will support your activities more if they have some say in how they are undertaken.

· Define objectives. Based upon member needs and community input, define those areas best addressed by an association. Set goals and objectives.

· Encourage volunteer support. Often there is no money for paid staff in the early days of an association. Volunteers will be critical to establish and operate the association, and maintain community support.

· Understand the structure of the organization. Most often an association will be a not-for-profit corporation which has specific characteristics and filing requirements. Make sure you are meeting all legal requirements.

· Secure financing. There will be costs for postage, photocopying, telephone, and travel. You may get donations and receive government grants for some costs. Likely you will need financial contributions from association members. Determine a reasonable fee and what will be provided to members in exchange. It will be a challenge to develop a fee structure that is affordable to a large number of businesses yet maintain the association.

· Establish ongoing communication. Continuing input from community stakeholders and prospective members is vital as is keeping these people informed.

Volunteers are critical in establishing and operating associations and maintaining community support.

WORKING WITHIN EXISTING TOURISM ASSOCIATIONS - Some nature-based tourism companies will prefer to work within existing tourism organizations instead of creating a new one. The State of California melds nature tourism into their regular tourism promotion as they feel it benefits from the same strategies and activities as other tourism sectors.

Convention and visitor bureaus, chambers of commerce, and guide associations all promote tourism and can provide benefits to members. The need to market a destination is common to all tourism-related businesses as are concerns surrounding customer service, taxation, and technology. Searching out organizations and becoming active in them will provide opportunities to market your ecotour or service. Seminars and workshops are often held on some aspects of business operations and marketing. Many organizations stress partnerships as a way to leverage marketing dollars, so it is possible that you will find non-ecotourism partners to expand your marketing efforts. Your results will be in proportion to your efforts.

The need to market a destination is common to all tourism-related businesses.

KEY POINTS

· Industry standards provide performance benchmarks against which ecotourism businesses are judged.
· Some businesses have used the green label as a marketing tool without adherence to environmental ethics. This creates confusion in the minds of the consumer.
· Some ecotourism standards have been created (Green Leaf, Green Globe, Eco Certification), yet are not widely recognized by consumers.
· Critics may doubt the integrity of ecotourism standards/certification financed by the ecotourism industry. Separation between financing and certification may be required to ensure meaningful standards.
· Tourism associations can provide benefits to ecotourism operators in terms of marketing and quality control.
· New ecotourism and nature-based tourism organizations are emerging in response to the growing number of operators and their concerns regarding marketing and operations.

WORKS CITED

1 Cecil, Harold Olaf, "The Search For Standards," *Travel Counselor,* pp. 16-24, October 1995.
2 Ibid.

IN CLOSING

The Business of Ecotourism has provided information on the many aspects of creating and running a business that is good for both the community and its owners. This provides a base to start your ecotourism operation or to improve an existing one. It is by no means the end of the road when it comes to learning about ecotourism. New consumer trends and changes in legislation will be challenging for organizations that sell travel products while protecting natural environments. Take these challenges as a call to stay involved in the industry and continue to learn as much as possible about new developments.

Join an association that represents your interests and stay actively involved. The International Ecotourism Society (TIES), The Adventure Travel Trade Association (ATTA), and The American Society of Travel Agents (ASTA) provide timely information to their members through newsletters and offer opportunities to network with other tourism operators. Local tourism organizations are important for information on regional trends, marketing activities, and planned changes to legislation. By staying informed, you will anticipate changes that could sidetrack your business. You can take steps to change your business or lobby governments for changes to legislation.

As ecotourism is still a new area within a fragmented industry, it is important to seek out others in this emerging field. By sharing information and working together we can accomplish more. We can protect our livelihoods from adverse legislative changes. Networking to create stronger businesses is important if we are going to establish a long-term place in the tourism industry and if ecotourism is going to set the standard for sustainable tourism. Only by defining environmentally-responsible tourism and working with tourism associations and government policy makers can we develop plans and legislation that will create sustainable businesses and environments.

Use *The Business of Ecotourism* as a springboard to broader activities. As you become more successful share your knowledge with others entering this field and use your acumen to work with decision makers in establishing regional and national policies. Above all, enjoy and respect what you do. By doing so, many years from now, you will still take the same pleasure in showing a person the beauty of an early morning on the trail.

APPENDIX A

BUSINESS PLANNING WORKBOOK

P.O. Box 46056, Inglewood P.O.   Calgary, Alberta, Canada, T2G 5H7   Tel: 403-290-0805

1.0 EXECUTIVE SUMMARY

1.1   Write an executive summary for your business including information on:

- · business description
- · products and services
- · sales and marketing
- · operating requirements
- · financial management

_____

_____

_____

_____

_____

_____

_____

_____

_____

_____

_____

_____

_____

_____

_____

_____

_____

_____

_____

_____

_____

_____

_____

_____

_____

_____

2.0 BUSINESS DESCRIPTION

2.1   Describe the basic nature of your business:

_____
_____
_____
_____
_____
_____
_____
_____
_____
_____

2.2   What year was your business founded? _____

2.3   What is the current form of business? If incorporated, what is the date/place of incorporation, classes of shares, number of shares authorized, issued, and outstanding? For a partnership identify partners and their respective percentage interest of the business.

_____
_____
_____
_____
_____
_____
_____
_____
_____
_____
_____
_____
_____
_____
_____
_____
_____
_____
_____
_____
_____

2.4   List the major events in your venture's history. Include any major obstacles the company has faced

   and accomplishments of the business.

_____

_____

_____

_____

_____

_____

_____

_____

_____

_____

_____

_____

_____

2.5   Describe the geographic region your business serves:

_____

_____

_____

_____

_____

_____

_____

_____

_____

_____

_____

_____

_____

2.6   Identify the key people in your business and their roles in the business:

_____

_____

_____

_____

_____

_____

_____

_____

_____

_____

_____

_____

2.7   What is your vision (where you want to be) for your company?

_____
_____
_____
_____
_____
_____
_____
_____
_____
_____
_____
_____
_____
_____
_____
_____
_____
_____
_____
_____
_____
_____
_____
_____

2.8   What is the mission (the purpose) of your business? What is your mission statement?

_____
_____
_____
_____
_____
_____
_____
_____
_____
_____
_____
_____
_____
_____
_____

2.9   List your business goals for the next three years:

_____

_____

_____

_____

_____

_____

_____

_____

_____

_____

_____

_____

_____

_____

_____

_____

_____

_____

_____

_____

_____

_____

_____

_____

_____

2.10   What are your objectives for the next six months?

_____

_____

_____

_____

_____

_____

_____

_____

_____

_____

_____

_____

_____

_____

_____

_____

3.0 PRODUCTS AND SERVICES

3.1   Describe the products and/or services your business provides:

_____
_____
_____
_____
_____
_____
_____
_____
_____
_____
_____
_____
_____
_____
_____
_____
_____
_____
_____
_____

3.2   What patents, trademarks, copyrights, proprietary features does your company hold?

_____
_____
_____
_____
_____
_____
_____
_____
_____
_____
_____
_____
_____
_____
_____
_____
_____
_____

3.3   What benefits do your products and services offer to your customers?

_____

_____

_____

_____

_____

_____

_____

_____

_____

_____

_____

_____

_____

3.4   List any key suppliers for you business:

_____

_____

_____

_____

_____

_____

_____

_____

_____

_____

_____

_____

_____

3.5   Describe any cooperative agreements you have with suppliers or other businesses e.g. cooperative marketing ventures:

_____

_____

_____

_____

_____

_____

_____

_____

_____

3.6   What future development are you planning and when?

_____
_____
_____
_____
_____
_____
_____
_____
_____
_____
_____
_____
_____
_____
_____
_____
_____
_____
_____
_____
_____
_____
_____
_____
_____

4.0   SALES AND MARKETING

4.1   Where is your business and industry in the product life cycle (i.e. new, growing, mature, declining)?

_____

_____

_____

_____

_____

_____

_____

_____

_____

_____

_____

_____

_____

_____

_____

_____

_____

_____

_____

_____

4.2   What characteristics describe your customer e.g. education, age, gender, geographic origin, income, occupation, interests?

_____

_____

_____

_____

_____

_____

_____

_____

_____

_____

_____

_____

_____

_____

_____

4.3   What market segments are you targeting?

_____
_____
_____
_____
_____
_____
_____
_____
_____
_____
_____
_____

4.4   Describe your competitors. What are their strengths and weaknesses?

_____
_____
_____
_____
_____
_____
_____
_____
_____
_____
_____

4.5   Identify your competitive advantage in the marketplace.

_____
_____
_____
_____
_____
_____
_____
_____
_____
_____
_____
_____

4.6   What pricing strategy will you use?

_____
_____
_____
_____
_____
_____
_____
_____
_____
_____
_____
_____
_____

4.7   List the advertising, public relations and promotional strategies you will use.

_____
_____
_____
_____
_____
_____
_____
_____
_____
_____
_____
_____
_____
_____
_____
_____
_____
_____
_____
_____
_____
_____
_____
_____
_____

4.8   What are the historical sales trends in your industry in recent years?

	20____	20____	20____
Number of units sold	_____	_____	_____
Sales	_____	_____	_____
Percentage change	_____	_____	_____

4.9   What are your forecasted sales (in units and $'s) for the next three years?

	20X1	20X2	20X3
Sales volume	_____	_____	_____
Sales revenue	_____	_____	_____

4.10   What guarantees will you offer with your product/service? What is your estimated cost of these guarantees?

_____

_____

_____

_____

_____

_____

_____

_____

_____

_____

_____

_____

_____

_____

_____

_____

_____

_____

_____

_____

5.0   OPERATIONS

5.1   What production processes are required to produce each of your products?

_____
_____
_____
_____
_____
_____
_____
_____
_____
_____
_____
_____
_____
_____
_____
_____
_____
_____
_____
_____

5.2   What number of staff are required to deliver your products and/or services to your customer? Identify the personnel by skill level.

_____
_____
_____
_____
_____
_____
_____
_____
_____
_____
_____
_____
_____
_____
_____
_____
_____

5.3 How many people-hours are available to your business (no. of people x hours worked by each person)? Do you have sufficient resources to service peak times? How will you handle periods of overstaffing e.g. beginning of season, shoulder season?

_____
_____
_____
_____
_____
_____
_____
_____
_____
_____
_____
_____
_____
_____
_____
_____
_____
_____
_____
_____
_____

5.4 Identify the equipment you require for your business and whether you will purchase or lease.

Equipment	Purchase or Lease	Cost	Lease Payment	Estimated Life

5.5   Describe the location of your business. Include information on site, ease of access, proximity to customers, size, signage, zoning, etc.

address: _____

size: _____

access: _____

proximity to customer: _____

signage: _____

length of lease: _____

cost: _____

proximity to suppliers: _____

labor availability: _____

5.6   What are the limitations of your present site?

_____
_____
_____
_____
_____
_____
_____
_____
_____
_____
_____
_____
_____
_____
_____
_____
_____
_____
_____
_____

5.7   What is the impact of government regulations on your business operations?

_____

_____

_____

_____

_____

_____

_____

_____

_____

_____

_____

_____

_____

_____

_____

_____

_____

_____

_____

_____

_____

5.8   Describe how the environmental impacts of your business will be minimized:

_____

_____

_____

_____

_____

_____

_____

_____

_____

_____

_____

_____

_____

_____

_____

5.9   What costs (or savings) will be incurred (realized) by your business as a result of activities from Sections 5.7 and 5.8?

_____
_____
_____
_____
_____
_____
_____
_____
_____
_____
_____
_____
_____
_____
_____
_____
_____
_____
_____
_____

5.10   Identify conservation groups (or types of groups) your business will support as part of its corporate strategy. What level and form of financial support is desirable?

_____
_____
_____
_____
_____
_____
_____
_____
_____
_____
_____
_____
_____
_____
_____
_____

5.11   What risks is your business exposed to? Identify your greatest risks.

1._____

2._____

3._____

4._____

5._____

6._____

7._____

5.12 Identify which kind of protection will work best for each type of risk:
- absorbing risk
- minimizing risk
- insuring against risks with commercial insurance

_____
_____
_____
_____
_____
_____
_____
_____
_____
_____
_____
_____
_____
_____
_____
_____
_____
_____
_____
_____
_____
_____
_____

5.13 Identify the insurance coverage required:

Type	Coverage Required	Premium Cost	Deductible
General liability			
Products or completed operations			
Fire and theft liability			
Business interruption			
Personal disability			
Key person			
Business loan			
Term life			
Medical			
Workers' Compensation			
Group			
Malpractice			

5.14   Describe the key players of the management team and their experience in the industry and in management.

5.15 Prepare an organizational chart for your business. Identify the major functional areas of your business. Add or move boxes as needed.

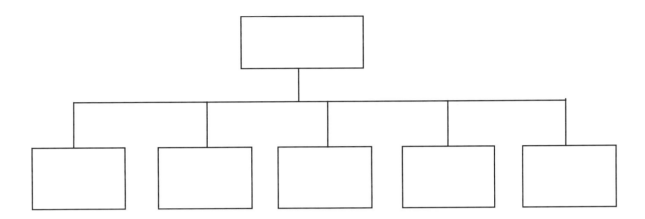

5.16 In which areas is your business strongest? Where does your business have weaknesses, either in lack of resources or level of expertise?

_____
_____
_____
_____
_____
_____
_____
_____
_____
_____
_____
_____
_____
_____
_____
_____
_____
_____
_____
_____

5.17   Which areas of your organization should you delegate or contract out? What kind of additional expertise would strengthen your business?

_____
_____
_____
_____
_____
_____
_____
_____
_____
_____
_____
_____
_____
_____
_____
_____
_____
_____
_____
_____
_____

5.18 What practices will be used to recruit staff? With whom does your business compete for people?

_____
_____
_____
_____
_____
_____
_____
_____
_____
_____
_____
_____
_____
_____
_____
_____

5.19   What training/incentives will be utilized to ensure customer service standards are met?

_____
_____
_____
_____
_____
_____
_____
_____
_____
_____
_____
_____
_____
_____
_____
_____

5.20   How competitive will your company be in benefits and wages offered to staff?

_____
_____
_____
_____
_____
_____
_____
_____
_____

5.21   Identify the method you will use to meet your human resource requirements:

Method	Number of People	Type of Work Performed
Permanent full-time employees		
Part-time employees		
Seasonal employees		
Consultants/contractors		

5.22   Identify the major activities your business will undertake and the time they will be completed:

Activity   Targeted Completion Date

_____
_____
_____
_____
_____
_____
_____
_____
_____
_____
_____
_____
_____
_____
_____
_____
_____
_____
_____
_____
_____
_____
_____
_____
_____
_____
_____
_____
_____
_____
_____
_____

6.0 FINANCIAL MANAGEMENT

6.1   Gather financial statements for the past three years if your business is an ongoing organization.

6.2   List the financial assumptions in your business plan.

Sales prices _____

Sales growth _____

Sales volumes _____

Time period to develop new customers _____

Material costs _____

Payroll _____

Debt financing requirements _____

Interest expense _____

General economic
conditions_____

6.3   Identify the start-up costs for your business or for your new products /or services.

Capital Expenditures:	**Amount $**
_____	_____
_____	_____
_____	_____
_____	_____
_____	_____
_____	_____
_____	_____

Marketing Costs:

_____   _____

_____   _____

_____   _____

_____   _____

Administration:

_____   _____

_____   _____

_____   _____

Legal: _____

Other: _____

TOTAL   **$**

6.4   Prepare a pro-forma income statement for your business for the next three years.

	20X1	20X2	20X3
Sales (by product/service):	_____	_____	_____
Cost of Sales:	_____	_____	_____
Gross Margin:	_____	_____	_____
Operating Expenses:	_____	_____	_____
Profit before Administration Expenses and Depreciation:	_____	_____	_____
Administration Expenses and Depreciation:	_____	_____	_____
Net Profit:	_____	_____	_____

6.5   Prepare a cash flow forecast for 12 months:

20xx CASH FLOW FORECAST

JAN FEB MAR APR MAY JUNE JULY AUG SEPT OCT NOV DEC

Cash On Hand

Cash Receipts
    New Investment
    Sales
    Bank Loan

Total Cash Receipts

Total Cash

Cash Disbursements
    Operating Expenses
    Bank Loan
    Insurance
    Withdrawals

Capital Expenditures
Total Cash Disbursements

Net Cash Flow

6.6   Prepare a pro-forma balance sheet for your business.

20X1

Current Assets

   Cash   _____

   Accounts Receivable   _____

   _____   _____

Total Current Assets   _____

   Equipment   _____

Total Assets   _____

Current Liabilities

   Accounts Payable   _____

   Bank Loan   _____

   Total Current Liabilities   _____

Long Term Debt   _____

Total Liabilities   _____

Owner's Equity   _____

Total Liabilities and Owner's Equity   _____

6.7   Calculate the break even point for your business or for your new product/service.

Sales   _____ _____

Fixed Costs   _____

Variable Costs   _____

1. Variable Cost per sales \$ = $\dfrac{\text{Variable Costs}}{\text{Sales}}$

_____

2. Contribution per sales \$ = \$1.00 -   _____

3. Break even point = $\dfrac{\text{Fixed Costs}}{\text{Contribution per sales \$}}$

_____

6.8   Identify the elements of your financial forecast that require sensitivity analysis:

e.g. sales price

_____

_____

_____

_____

_____

6.9   What rate of return will you be able to offer investors?

ROI = $\dfrac{\text{Net Income}}{\text{Owner's Equity}}$ =   _____ / _____

=   _____

6.10   Prepare a personal net worth statement.

General Information:

Dependents including spouse _____

Salary or wages _____

Other income _____

Guarantees on debts of others _____

Assets:

Bank accounts _____

Stocks _____

RRSP _____

Home _____

Automobile _____

Other

_____   _____

_____   _____

_____   _____

Total Assets: _____

Liabilities:

Bank loan _____

Charge accounts _____

Mortgage payments _____

Other

_____   _____

_____   _____

Total Liabilities: _____

Net Worth: ....

6.10   Prepare a personal estimate of monthly living costs.

Income:

        Salary or wages (all family members)   _____

        Other income   _____

        Total Income: _____

Expenses:

        Rent/mortgage   _____

        Electricity   _____

        Heating   _____

        Telephone   _____

        Insurance (car, house, life)   _____

        Taxes (property, municipal)   _____

        Food   _____

        Medication   _____

        Clothing   _____

        School fees   _____

        Gifts (Christmas, birthday)   _____

        Entertainment   _____

        Car payments   _____

        Car repairs and expense   _____

        Other   _____

        Total Expenses: _____

    Net Monthly Surplus (shortfall):   _____

6.11   Identify financing requirements.

Project Cost	$	Source of Funds	$
_____	_____	_____	_____
_____	_____	_____	_____
_____	_____	_____	_____
_____	_____	_____	_____
_____	_____	_____	_____

6.12   What strategy will be used to attract investors?

_____
_____
_____
_____
_____
_____
_____
_____
_____

BUSINESS PLAN APPENDICES

1. List the information you will include in your business plan appendices.

_____
_____
_____
_____
_____
_____
_____
_____
_____
_____
_____
_____
_____
_____
_____

APPENDIX B

Creating A Tourism Career From Scratch

I did it. You can do it too. When I started in the tourism field few people knew what ecotourism was. Many confused it with eco-terrorism! I had been working as an accounting supervisor at an oil and gas company when I decided it was time for me to combine my love of travel and wildlife into a career.

There were no manuals to point the way and there were few jobs in the field. None in the city, Calgary, that I chose to call home. But I stumbled upon a delightful book, *Wishcraft* by Barbara Sher that explained how you could take what you loved and turn it into a living. I was hooked by the concept and while it wasn't easy, I kept at it. I talked to anyone who could tell me more about this emerging field and I spent hours considering how my business skills could be transferred into a field abounding with biologists, policy wonks, public relation's experts, and marketing professionals.

One of my earliest successes was this book. In writing *The Business of Ecotourism* I was able to translate key planning concepts into practical advice needed by people wanting to succeed in the field of nature or cultural tourism. The people I've met in the field of nature tourism have a passion for the outdoors, not for their general ledgers or business plans. *The Business of Ecotourism* helped me carve a niche as a conduit of information to help people succeed as sustainable tourism operators without being chained to their laptop.

I am going to share with you the tools that helped me create a career in tourism when there were few signposts to guide the way. Chances are you are looking for work in a field that is still developing in your community. In looking for work that gives you time outdoors and reasonable pay, you may have run into a dead-end reading the want ads or searching the Internet. I'll share what I've learned and help you find the way.

You may be disappointed with some of what you discover in your search and you will probably work harder than you've ever worked before, but if you preserve you **will** find a way to combine your life's passions and a living. Let's get started!

What Do You Want To Do?

Creating a career in tourism, especially in the field of ecotourism or nature tourism, will require you to be creative, persistent and clever. You will also need to build a level of self-awareness so you can find the opportunities that are most likely to keep you happy.

Everyone has different interests and the trick will be finding a money-making opportunity connected to yours. There will be more possibilities that you might think. You may have to discard some of them based upon your family situation or your tolerance for risk, but for now focus on what you want to have more of in your life.

Start by listing your goals. What do you want to get out of your career in tourism? A chance to spend more time engaged in a favorite recreational activity? More time outdoors? These are common goals, but make sure to consider what type of people you hope to include in these goals. If you want to spend more time canoeing, are you ready to do with it with people who don't know an eddy from a riptide? Many people are surprised at how little time they actually have left over for their sport once they have taken care of the customer safety briefing, equipment selection, training tips, orientation and overall customer service.

Will you want to work for someone else or are you prepared to take on the risks of self-employment? Lots of people envy the flexibility of a business owner, but overlook the hours that go into getting a business up and running. Be honest about the time and energy you can commit to getting your new career established.

Where do you want to spend your time? Is it important for you to be located in a certain part of the country? Are you mobile? Many tourism businesses are seasonal and you will have to find something to do in the off season. One option may be to do the same thing, but in a different hemisphere. Paddling guides have been doing this for years. After leading trips in North America all summer, they relocate to Central America or south-east Asia for the winter months.

To help clarify what you want in a career, try answering the following questions:

My goals for a career in tourism are:

1._____

2._____

3._____

4._____

5._____

The kind of people I would like to work with include: (describe each briefly)

Customers:

_____

Coworkers:

_____

Boss:

_____

I would like to do the following types of tasks and activities:

1. _____

2. _____

3. _____

4. _____

What type of physical environment do you want to work in?

_____

What work hours would you prefer? Do you like shift work? Long hours? Flexibility?

_____

What level of income do you need to cover your living expenses? If you are married, have you discussed your income goals with your partner to make sure they support your goals and expectations?

_____

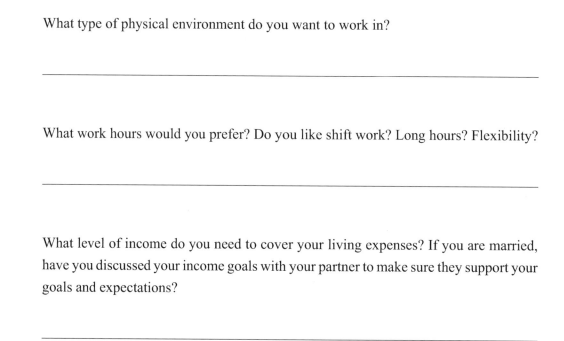

Need Help Figuring Out What You Want To Do?

The books I've listed below can be invaluable in helping you define a great tourism career. If you are a midlife career changer you have lots of transferable work skills and experiences, but you will also want to build a job that includes your special interests and your passions. Unfortunately, raising a family and building your first career may have knocked all the passion right out of you.

For those in that category, I recommend you take these books to the beach or the mountains (or the bathroom with the door locked) and create some quiet time before you try setting your goals. You need time to remember what you love to do, not just what you are good at doing. Sometimes they are the same, but often there is a part of you that is screaming for more expression. Working in tourism is a great venue for letting that creativity out.

Tourism is still a field where what you can do counts more than what you've studied so you are only limited by your imagination, time and energy.

Great Books To Help You Find Your Tourism Calling:
Wishcraft by Barbara Sher
Refuse to Choose by Barbara Sher
What Color is Your Parachute? By Richard Nelson Bolles

Are You Ready For The Challenges?

Defining your goals will often take several days or weeks as you mull over your options and find the time to answer the earlier questions completely and honestly. Once you have a general idea of what you would like to do, start investigating the jobs and business opportunities found in ecotourism and nature tourism.

Table 1–1 in Chapter One gives you the multitude of organizations that form this industry. You will find that there are many jobs in the public sector working for government as well as those private businesses dealing directly with travelers. If you are deeply concerned about social or environmental causes you might like working with a non-profit or non-government organization (NGO). See **Some Definitions** for more information about the different types of organizations involved in tourism.

Some Definitions

Private sector – These are organizations set up to generate a profit. Often they are incorporated organizations which have limited liability for owners (see Chapter 11 for more details on corporate structures)

Public sector – This sector includes municipal, provincial, state and federal governments with a mandate to deliver services for the common good. Those government departments that will often have a connection to tourism include Fish and Wildlife, resource management, tourism development and marketing, human resources, training and education, economic development, agricultural diversification, rural development, etc.

Non-governmental organizations (NGOs) - NGOs are non profit organizations whose mandate is of a social, political or environmental nature. They may be a charitable organization although not all NGOs are registered charities. They may have a tourism component to their programs if tourism is seen as a valuable tool in achieving their goals.

Some of the career paths in ecotourism may be obvious, such as being a kayak guide or running a B&B catering to bird watchers, but there are other careers that you may have overlooked. Insurance agents, accountants, lawyers and other professionals are also needed in this part of the tourism industry. You might want to consider working in one of these fields and specializing in environmental or ecotourism matters.

Do an inventory of all the organizations in your community that may have a connection to ecotourism or nature tourism. You can use the inventory in Figure 2-2 to get started. When you get to the sections on tourism attractions and facilities try to list some of the organizations operating in your area. These may be potential employers, but equally as important they will have people that can provide useful information for your career search.

Once you've completed the tourism inventory for your community or the one in which you would like to work, spend some time on the Internet. Visit the websites of the organizations that interest you. Learn about their goals and the types of activities they undertake. Read their press releases or online newsletters. What type of challenges do they face? Showing up with solutions to these problems can give you an instant leg-up in establishing your career.

After you've investigated a dozen different organizations summarize your thoughts below:

Which organizations were most interesting?

1. _____

2. _____

3. _____

4. _____

5. _____

What aspects of these organizations did I like the most?

1. _____

2. _____

3. _____

4. _____

Where there any things these organizations had in common? For example, were they all committed to delivering unusual adventures? Did they focus on fun and exciting times for young people? Was there an aspect of conservation that excited you? Try to summarize those elements that struck a chord with you.

_____

What common challenges did you see with these organizations? For example, were many of them looking to attract younger customers or wanting to expand their shoulder season activities?

_____

What ideas do you have on how these organizations can beat these challenges?

_____

What Do You Bring To The Party?

Now that you have a better idea of what you want to do and the types of organizations that interest you, it is time to look at what you can offer.

This can be a difficult process for some people. They may feel that they have no applicable skills or training. I can relate to that. Trained as a professional accountant I wasn't sure my skills would be valued in the ecotourism field. However, I had been building bridges to a new career without realizing it and I suspect you have too!

For a number of years before my career change I had been indulging my passion for wildlife by being a volunteer guide at the Calgary Zoo. I had developed new skills in the area of interpretation, public speaking and wildlife viewing. With my understanding of the newly emerging field of ecotourism, I could see that many organizations needed people with good communication skills, knowledge of business processes, and an interest in people. Those were things I could provide and I'm sure you will find that you have skills in your past that can be 'repackaged' to create the career you want in tourism.

Start by listing those skills you possess that will be of immediate value in the tourism industry. This might include any certifications, diplomas or licenses you've picked up in your pursuit of your passion.

_____

Add to the list the outdoor skills you have that do not come with certifications. Lots of tourism organizations need people with specialized knowledge to add interest to their customers' trips so if you are a crack birder or have the aboriginal history of your community researched, write it down. You would be amazed at how many people are looking for someone with your background even if it is on a part-time basis.

_____

List any degrees, diplomas or certifications you hold even if they aren't directly related to tourism. You may be able to find a way to link your knowledge to the field of tourism or do some online training to add a tourism specialization.

_____

Tourism employers have told me time and again that they can teach an employee almost anything, but they can't teach a person to smile. If you have the ability to chitchat with people or make them feel comfortable in a social situation, you will do well in tourism. These 'soft' skills are often the most important in determining your overall success in tourism.

List those skills or attributes you possess that may help you with your tourism career. Be sure to include your ability to organize, remain calm under pressure, build entire structures using duct tape and one fallen tree, etc.

_____

Tell Me More

At this point you have a good idea of what you can contribute to a tourism organization and you have some idea of your goals. It's time for you to get out and find out more about tourism jobs in your community. You are about to start on the informational interviewing process.

This wonderful tool is identified by Richard Nelson Bolles in *What Color is Your Parachute?* He describes the **single** most important tool you can use in your career building process. Want to find out more about tourism jobs in your field? Use information interviews. What to find out who might be hiring? Use information interviews. Want to find out what associations the movers and shakers belong to? Use information interviews.

The premise of an information interview is that you ask a tourism professional for fifteen to twenty minutes of their time to get their expert opinion on a number of issues you are researching. It is not a job search!!! You want to find out more about the tourism field before you decide which organizations are worthy of your time, talents and a copy of your resume.

Go to these interviews with questions on the main issues facing these organizations, what types of skills their employees possess, what they are missing and which trade associations they belong to. This will help you understand how to best position your skills **before** you apply for a job. You may decide based upon your informational interviews that you have been looking in the wrong places and need to redirect your search or develop new skills.

Start by identifying five people with who you would like to conduct an informational interview. Ask everyone you know for the names of anyone remotely associated with ecotourism and call them up for appointments. Explain carefully why you want to see them so they don't mistake you for a job hunter. Eventually you will be looking for work, but at this point you are just researching your options.

Conduct your informational interviews. Respect people's time and keep to the 20 minutes originally requested. Send a thank you note. It will help you build your new career network. If you are having trouble finding people in your community with the career you want to emulate, look further afield. Sometimes people are more willing to share information with someone located at a distance because they are less likely to be seen as a competitor.

What observations can you make about the field of tourism since you concluded your interviews?

Has your research given you ideas on what your future career might look like? Describe what form your career possibilities might take. Will this be a job in the conventional sense or will it be a variety of jobs linked together to give you the income you need? Chances are you will be working with a number of employers to create year round employment or you may be creating a business to provide yourself with self-employment income.

What other information do you need before you apply for work or start a business? Do you need to research zoning guidelines? Find out which paddling certifications are offered in your community? Make a list of things you need to know and where you might get the information.

Making Friends and Building Your Network

Hopefully the informational interviewing process showed you the value of networking and you added a few names to your address book. If not, now is the time to build a professional network. Tourism is an industry made up of extremely social individuals. Your ability to succeed in this field will be determined to a large extent by how good you are at building relationships with people. While you are building your career prospects, take the time to build the network that will generate the job offers or business partnerships you will need for success.

Your Internet research and information interviews should have revealed which associations the people in your field belong to. Join up and be prepared to go their annual conferences. Conferences are a great place to build your network. It is a low stress, fun-filled way to meet people and organizers often have special student's rates if you are still finishing off your education. I know of lots of people, myself included, who have gotten major breaks through the casual connections made at tourism conferences.

Finding the Opportunity

Now it is time to start looking for the job of your dreams. Using the information you gathered in your informational interviews, decide how you can help organizations solve their problems. The fact that you have taken the time to research their company and suggest success strategies will set you far above the competition.

Call your contacts and tell them what type of job you are now looking for. Don't be shy. Tell everyone what type of position you want AND what you have to offer. Your information interviews will have given you a much better idea of which companies you want to work for. You will also have a clearer idea of what skills employers are looking for. Chances are you will also have personal contacts that can keep your resume from disappearing in the Human Resource's pool of unsolicited applicants.

You may decide that working for someone else is not for you. Many people in the field of ecotourism and adventure travel will decide to start their own businesses. If this option interests you, consider working for a similar business to gain some experience before you invest your savings in a business. Once you've seen how ecotourism businesses operate, you can move forward with your ides. The Business of Ecotourism will help you create the vision and the business plan you need to develop your concept further.

Don't get discouraged. It will take time to land the perfect job or build a business. You may need to start with a less than perfect job and work your way into the position or company of your dreams. Having a good attitude while you 'earn your stripes' will endear you to employers and make your journey go much faster. If it helps, read motivational books or watch motivational tapes. A favorite of mine is found at www.thesecret.tv. Looking for work is the hardest job there is, so be kind to yourself. Things will come together if you are persistent.

Increasing Your Chances of Success

When you are building your new career in ecotourism recognize that it will take time to become established in a manner seen in more traditional fields. Very few people work year round in this field. Most people have secondary sources of income in the off season. Some people take their marketing expertise and design websites for other companies.

Some people find complementary outdoor jobs with lots of flexibility like firefighting. Others look for work they can do from home, for example, building furniture.

Give some thought to the types of work you might be able to do in your slow times. Are there skills you already possess that can generate extra income? Are there certifications or licenses you can get that will provide you with financial security when tourism goes through down cycles?

_____

Don't feel that you have failed if you need to find other ways to support your true passions while you establish yourself in the tourism field. Many people spend years building up their tourism businesses to the point where they can rely on it for their annual livelihood. Having another source of income can give you the time needed to realize your career dreams in the field of tourism. If you keep at it, one day people will be telling you they envy your lifestyle. Even though you will be working like a demon, you'll look up and realize that you've made it!

Giving Back

Building your tourism career will require the help of others. As I've suggested, asking established tourism professionals for information interviews will be an important part of your strategy. Some people will be extremely generous of their time and help you make contacts that will prove invaluable. Remember to 'pay it forward'. Once you've got your toe-hold established in the tourism field, take the time to help others follow their dreams.

If someone calls you for an informational interview, help them if you can. Give a student the chance to work for you on a co-op work term. Donate your time to a tourism industry association. Doing these things will strengthen the ecotourism industry and help us build an industry with passionate, talented individuals.

Be sure as well to take time to recharge and spend time in nature. You will find creating your tourism career time-consuming and there is a temptation to give up some of your favorite outdoor activities. Make it a priority to get back to the woods, mountains, desert or waters that turned you on to nature tourism in the first place. You'll be happier and your contribution to the tourism industry will be greater!

I leave you a closing thought by John Muir

"Climb the mountains and get their good tidings.
Nature's peace will flow into you as sunshine flows into trees.
The winds will blow their own freshness into you...
while cares will drop off like autumn leaves."

215

INDEX

217

Made in the USA
Columbia, SC
25 February 2019